Psychoanalytic Ecology

Psychoanalytic Ecology applies Freudian concepts, beginning with the uncanny, to environmental issues, such as wetlands and their loss, to alligators and crocodiles as inhabitants of wetlands, and to the urban underside. It also applies other Freudian concepts, such as sublimation, symptom, mourning and melancholia, to environmental issues and concerns. Mourning and melancholia can be experienced in relation to wetlands and to their loss. The city is a symptom of the will to fill or drain wetlands.

This book engages in a talking cure of psychogeopathology (environmental psychopathology; mental land illness; environ-mental illness) manifested also in industries, such as mining and pastoralism, that practice greed and gluttony. *Psychoanalytic Ecology* promotes gratitude for generosity as a way of nurturing environ-mental health to prevent the manifestation of these psychogeopathological symptoms in the first place. Melanie Klein's work on anal sadism is applied to mining and Karl Abraham's work on oral sadism to pastoralism. Finally, Margaret Mahler's and Jessica Benjamin's work on psycho-symbiosis is drawn on to nurture bio- and psycho-symbiotic livelihoods in bioregional home-habitats of the living earth in the symbiocene, the hoped-for age superseding the Anthropocene.

Psychoanalytic Ecology demonstrates the power of psychoanalytic concepts and the pertinence of the work of several psychoanalytic thinkers for analysing a range of environmental issues and concerns. This book will be of great interest to students and scholars of environmental psychology, psychoanalysis and the environmental humanities.

Rod Giblett is Honorary Associate Professor of Environmental Humanities in the School of Communication and Creative Arts, Deakin University, Australia. He is the author of many books in the environmental humanities, including *People and Places of Nature and Culture* (2011) and most recently, *Environmental Humanities and Theologies* (2018), and is a pioneer in psychoanalytic ecology.

Routledge Focus on Environment and Sustainability

For more information about this series, please visit: www.routledge.com/
Routledge-Focus-on-Environment-and-Sustainability/book-series/RFES

Psychoanalytic Ecology

The Talking Cure for Environmental Illness and Health

Rod Giblett

LONDON AND NEW YORK

First published 2019
by Routledge
2 Park Square, Milton Park, Abingdon, Oxon OX14 4RN

and by Routledge
52 Vanderbilt Avenue, New York, NY 10017

First issued in paperback 2020

Routledge is an imprint of the Taylor & Francis Group, an informa business

British Library Cataloguing-in-Publication Data
A catalogue record for this book is available from the British Library

Library of Congress Cataloging-in-Publication Data
Names: Giblett, Rodney James, author.
Title: Psychoanalytic ecology : the talking cure for environmental illness
    and health / Rod Giblett.
Description: Abingdon, Oxon ; New York, NY : Routledge, 2019. |
    Series: Routledge focus on environment and sustainability | Includes
    bibliographical references and index.
Identifiers: LCCN 2018056477 | ISBN 9780367181536 (hardback : alk.
    paper) | ISBN 9780429059797 (e-book)
Subjects: LCSH: Environmental psychology. | Environmental
    degradation—Psychological aspects.
Classification: LCC BF353 .G53 2019 | DDC 155.9/1—dc23
LC record available at https://lccn.loc.gov/2018056477

ISBN 13: 978-0-367-67023-8 (pbk)
ISBN 13: 978-0-367-18153-6 (hbk)

Typeset in Times New Roman
by Apex CoVantage, LLC

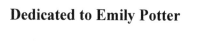

Dedicated to Emily Potter

Contents

Acknowledgements

Psychoanalytic ecology and this book had its beginnings in the amazing interdisciplinary context of Murdoch University in the 1980s and the supportive environment of Curtin University in the early/mid 1990s. I am grateful to the following friends and colleagues who were at either university at the time:

Zoë Sofoulis for generously allowing me access to her PhD thesis from UCLA Santa Cruz and to Maria Angel for pointing out its pertinence; Zoë also for making copies of her other work available to me, for discussions of the sublime, slime and the uncanny, and for drawing my attention to the work of Melanie Klein;

Alec McHoul for drawing my attention to Immanuel Kant's early work, *Observations on the Feeling of the Beautiful and Sublime*;

Ann McGuire and Jon Stratton for pointing out, respectively, the pertinence of Spengler's and Simmel's work to mine;

Rita Felski for alerting me to the fact that Bachofen's work was available in an English translation and that a copy was housed in the Murdoch University Library;

Bethany Broun for pointing out to me the pertinence of Camille Paglia's *Sexual Personae*;

Cheryl Gole for drawing my attention to Lacan's account of the symptom;

Bob Hodge for a unit I taught with him and Zoë Sofoulis entitled 'Language, Culture and the Unconscious' at Murdoch University in the late 1980s for alerting me to the cultural possibilities of Freud's theory of symptom; and

Mudrooroo and Hugh Webb for making the former's 'report' on mining operations in the Pilbara region of Western Australia available to me.

Psychoanalytic ecology and this book developed in the late 1990s, 2000s and early 2010s at Edith Cowan University. I am grateful to Susan Ash for pointing out the pertinence of Jessica Benjamin's *The Bonds of Love*. Beginning at ECU and since leaving ECU at the end of 2014, psychoanalytic ecology continued its development in *Cities and Wetlands: The Return of the Repressed in Nature and Culture* (Bloomsbury, 2016). *Psychoanalytic Ecology* brings together work ranging from the late 1980s to the late 2010s in *Environmental Humanities and Theologies* (Routledge, 2018). *Psychoanalytic Ecology* thus reflects on thirty years in the development of psychoanalytic ecology. No doubt, *Psychoanalytic Ecology* is not the end of the story; it is only the beginning. Other psychoanalytic thinkers and writers, such as Sabina Spielrein whose work is now more easily accessible for English-speaking readers with the publication of her 'essential writings' so that she is no longer a forgotten pioneer of psychoanalysis, may provide further avenues for developing psychoanalytic ecology. I look forward to reading them. Others may find different avenues for developing psychoanalytic ecology. I look forward to reading them too.

Writing *Psychoanalytic Ecology* and preparing it for publication were performed in the supportive context of the Writing and Literature Program in the School of Communication and Creative Arts at Deakin University. I am grateful to Emily Potter for her invitation to apply for an honorary appointment at Deakin and to join the 'Shadow Places' Network; hence the dedication of this book to her. I am also grateful to Lyn McCredden for supporting my application, guiding it through the approval process and launching some previous books.

1 Psychoanalytic ecology and the uncanny

Sigmund Freud's work on the uncanny, sublimation, symptom, mourning and melancholia is the basis for psychoanalytic ecology. For Freud, symptoms of psychopathology are inscribed on the surface of the patient's, or analysand's, body; for psychoanalytic ecology, symptoms of psychogeopathology are inscribed on the surface of the earth. Psychogeopathology is the mental illness associated with what Aldo Leopold (1991, pp. 212–217), a pioneer of conservation, called 'land pathology.' For Freud, symptoms of psychopathology are removed through the 'talking cure' that resolves the causes of the symptoms. Along similar lines, psychoanalytic ecology diagnoses the symptoms, and engages in a talking cure, of the psychogeopathology of the will to fill or drain wetlands, the uncanny place *par excellence*. The first chapter of *Psychoanalytic Ecology* draw on Freud's work to discuss the psychodynamics of these processes.

Wetlands are sometimes not, and sometimes not ever, the most pleasant of places. In Western aesthetics they are not beautiful, sublime nor picturesque. They are anti-aesthetic, bodily, repressed and sublimated. Wetlands have been also associated with melancholia, or depression, especially 'the slough of despond' beginning with John Bunyan's *Pilgrim's Progress* first published in 1678 (Bunyan, 2008). Freud also associated melancholia with mourning as the loss of a loved object of love (Freud, 2005). Melancholia also involves a loss of the subject. Wetlands are a lost source of sustenance and entail a lost subject. The second chapter of *Psychoanalytic Ecology* draws on Freud's work on mourning and melancholia to discuss the psychodynamics of love and loss of subjects and objects.

Alligators and crocodiles as monstrous creatures for Freud are vehicles and vectors for the uncanny. The uncanny urban underside is a fascinating and horrifying place for Freud. Freud's work on the uncanny is drawn on more specifically in chapters 3 and 4 of *Psychoanalytic Ecology*. These two chapters diagnose the symptoms, and engage in a talking cure, of the psychogeopathology of demonizing and discriminating against these creatures and places. Placial discrimination and placism operate like racial discrimination and racism. Not only is there a hierarchy of places and races in which one race and place is privileged over all others, but also the 'superior' race figures the 'inferior' race and place in pejorative terms, for example, the slum as swamp (and vice versa), the 'native' as 'primitive.'

The mining and pastoral (sheep- and cattle-grazing) industries exact oral and anal sadism against the earth. The work of Melanie Klein and Karl Abraham are used to diagnose the symptoms, and engage in a talking cure, of the psychogeopathology of oral and anal sadism in chapters 5 and 6 of *Psychoanalytic Ecology*. These chapters critique resource-exploitation, or greed and gluttony, and argue for a relationship of generosity for gratitude, of respect for, reciprocity with, and restoration of the earth to promote environ-mental health. Rather than just diagnose the symptoms and engage in a talking cure of them, psychoanalytic ecology nurtures environ-mental health and prevents the development and manifestation of the symptoms of psychogeopathology in the first place. The work of Margaret Mahler and Jessica Benjamin on psycho-symbiosis are used to do so in the final chapter. It also draws on the work of Lynn Margulis and Michel Serres on parasitism and symbiosis. Psycho-symbiosis is mental health associated with what Leopold (1999, p. 219; see also 1949, p. 221) called 'land health.' It nurtures living with the earth in the symbiocene, the hoped-for age superseding the Anthropocene.

The uncanny

The uncanny is the obverse of sublimation. Freud used the metaphor of sublimation drawn from chemistry to describe the process of sublimation by which sexual desire is displaced or deflected into ostensibly non-sexual realms, particularly the aesthetic and the intellectual (Freud, 1985a, pp. 39, 41, 45; see also Laplanche and Pontalis, 1973, pp. 431–434). The sublime and sublimation are closely linked as Immanuel Kant (1960, p. 57) attests that the sublimation of 'subduing one's passions through principles is sublime.' The sublimation of sexuality into the aesthetic and intellectual are part of the condition of modernity, especially in the light of Simmel's and Spengler's argument that the intellect developed in conjunction with the rise of the modern metropolis (Simmel, 1950, pp. 409–424). Indeed, for Spengler (1932, p. 96; see also p. 92), 'the city is intellect.' The city, sublimation and the intellect come together in what Norman O. Brown (1959, pp. 281–283) calls 'the city sublime,' especially the modern city.

Yet, despite, or perhaps because of, the triumphs of modernity sublimation is always haunted by its shadow, its 'other.' The sublime, Zoë Sofoulis suggests, is always shadowed by the uncanny. Rather than the reverse of the sublime, for Sofoulis (1988, p. 12) 'the uncanny is the obverse of the sublime, its other side: that from which it springs and that into which its turns,' and even that into which it *re*turns (Figure 1.1, p. 4 below). Sofoulis (1988, p. 15, n. 86) goes on to suggest that the uncanny is associated with slime, and that 'slime is the secret of the sublime,' which she encapsulates in the paren-thetical portmanteau 's(ub)lime.' The home, or perhaps more precisely the 'unhome,' of the slimy, and the uncanny, is the wetland summed up in the reference to 'the slime of the swamplands' (Tremayne, 1985, p. 150). The wetland is the uncanny place *par excellence.*

The concept/metaphor of the uncanny is arguably the greatest and most fruitful contribution of Freud to the study of culture and nature. Freud developed the uncanny in his essay of this title first published in 1919 in the psychoanalytic journal *Imago.* It was translated into English by Alix Strachey in 1925 for Freud's *Collected Papers.* This translation was then 'considerably modified' for her husband's James's *Standard Edition of the Complete Psychological Works of Sigmund Freud* and republished by Penguin in their 'Penguin Freud Library' sixty years later (Freud, 1985b). A new translation was commissioned and published by Penguin early this century (Freud, 2003).

Although a whole swag of Freud's concepts and ideas (such as the Oedi-pus complex, penis envy, and so on) are critiqued and problematized, or pooh-poohed and dismissed as the years go on, the uncanny endures for a century as a useful tool in the toolbox of cultural criticism, literary the-ory, and political and philosophical critique. Freud (1919, p. 219; cf. 2003, p. 124) defines the uncanny as 'that class of the frightening which leads back to what is known of old and long familiar.' This is specifically, though Freud does not mention it, what Randolph (2001b, p. 97) calls 'the mother-infant embrace,' both *in-utero* and *ex-utero.* For Freud (1919, p. 244, 2003, p. 151) the uncanny is literally *unheimlich,* unhomely, but also homely, con-tradictory feelings which he found associated in the minds of adult males with female genitalia and in his own mind with the first home of individ-ual human life in the mother's womb. The uncanny entails a return of the repressed.

The return of the repressed occurs here and elsewhere for Freud as he does not refer to the mother – his or anybody else's – or to her body, or specifically her womb. The maternal body is repressed in and by Freud in his essay on the uncanny as Randolph (2001a, p. 184, 2001b, p. 97) points out. The maternal body is repressed in and by patriarchal Western culture more generally (Giblet 1996, p. 6). Freud's uncanny is uncanny in which the repressed maternal body returns. Freud (2003, p. 151) relates that 'it often happens that neurotic men state that to them there is something uncanny

A PSYCHOGEOCORPOGRAPHY OF MODERNITY

© Rod Giblett, 1994.

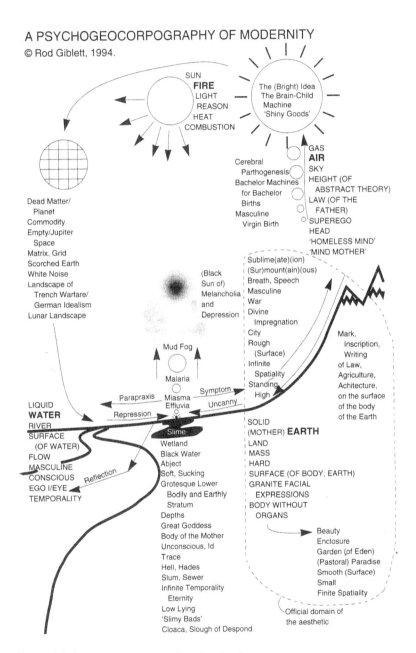

Figure 1.1 A pyschogeocorpography of modernity

about the female genital organs. But what they find uncanny ["unhomely"] is actually the entrance to man's old "home," the place where everyone once lived.' Freud is, of course, referring to the womb, but seems a bit squeamish about doing so explicitly. 'Man's' old home is the womb, whereas the old men's home is (the entrance to) the tomb. The womb is more than a place (where action occurs, or a site where action takes place; it is not a passive receptacle). It is where the processes of life begin and are nurtured. It is also where the first bond occurs *in-utero* and the mother's body is where the first bond occurs *ex-utero*.

Life *in-utero* is a time and space when, as Freud (1919, p. 235; cf. 2003, p. 143) describes it euphemistically, 'the ego had not yet marked itself off sharply from the external world and from other people.' Freud (1919, p. 235) goes on to remark that 'these factors are partly responsible for the impression of uncanniness.' Both Freud's euphemisms of 'the external world' and 'other people' for the mother's body are factors partly responsible for the impression of uncanniness in Freud's essay on the uncanny. Life *in-utero* and *ex-utero* is a time and space when the ego had not set itself against anything, including the external world, and from other people, such as the mother. The mother herself, as Randolph (2001b, p. 98) puts it following Klein, is 'the infant's "external world"' and the 'other people' Freud vaguely refers to is the mother. The ego was a part and parcel of the inside world *in-utero* and the uncanny other, the mother, and of the outside world *ex-utero*. In 1919 in 'The Uncanny' Freud misses 'the whole point about mothering' as Randolph (2001a, p. 186) puts it. Twenty years later in his London notes of 1938 Freud (1975, p. 299) gets closer to the point about mothering by mimicking the child: 'the breast is a part of me, I am the breast.' All objects are initially conflated with one another and equated with the mother, or parts of her, especially her breasts, as she/they are the primary object for the young infant. Klein, as Randolph (2001b, p. 98) puts it, 'gave the mother her due,' as Mahler did too in her work on psycho-symbiosis and Jessica Benjamin in her work on 'the bonds of love' (and discussed in the final chapter of *Psychoanalytic Ecology*).

The home place and processes, or perhaps more precisely the 'unhome,' of the uncanny is not only the mother's womb, but also the wetland, the first home of life on the planet in the earth's womb and tomb from both of which new life springs and is nurtured (see Giblett, 1996, chapter 2; 2018, chapter 1). Wetlands are vital for life on earth, including human and non-human life. The leading intergovernmental agency on wetlands states that:

> they are among the world's most productive environments; cradles of biological diversity that provide the water and productivity upon which countless species of plants and animals depend for survival. Wetlands

are indispensable for the countless benefits or "ecosystem services" that they provide humanity, ranging from freshwater supply, food and building materials, and biodiversity, to flood control, groundwater recharge, and climate change mitigation. Yet study after study demonstrates that wetland area[s] and [their] quality continue to decline in most regions of the world. As a result, the ecosystem services that wetlands provide to people are compromised.

(Ramsar Convention Bureau, online)

Yet more than the mere providers of 'ecosystem services,' wetlands are habitats for plants and animals, and homes for people.

The wetland is the uncanny place and process *par excellence*. It is also the home, or unhome, of alligators and crocodiles, the 'king' of the tropical wetland, the obverse of the temperate dry land, and the archetypal swamp monsters *par excellence* (discussed in chapter 3 of *Psychoanalytic Ecology*). In his 1919 essay on the uncanny Freud relates how:

I read a story about a young married couple who move into a furnished house in which there is a curiously shaped table with carvings of crocodiles on it. Towards evening an intolerable and very specific smell begins to pervade the house; they stumble over something in the dark; they seem to see a vague form gliding over the stairs – in short we are given to understand that the presence of the table causes ghostly crocodiles to haunt the place, or that the wooden monsters come to life in the dark, or something of that sort.

(Freud, 1985b, p. 367)

Freud's account of the uncanny is crucial for a number of points. In the story the uncanny is produced by the smell of virtual crocodiles, the 'king' of the tropical wetland, the obverse of the temperate dry land, and the archetypal swamp monster *par excellence* as well as for John Ruskin 'slime-begotten' (as cited in the *Oxford English Dictionary* entry under 'slime'). The crocodile is not the only creature slime-begotten. Slime is, as Camille Paglia (1991, p. 11) puts it, also for humans 'our site of biologic origins.' The story is also significant because of its emphasis on the sense of smell. It is no surprise then to find that Hoffmann (1982, p. 88), that master of the uncanny for Freud, in 'The Sandman,' the story in which Freud found the uncanny most powerfully evoked, should also refer to 'a subtle, strange-smelling vapour . . . spreading through the house.' For Freud the uncanny is *unheimlich*, unhomely, but also homely, contradictory feelings which Freud found associated with the first home of the womb in the minds of adult males.

The uncanny counters the aesthetics of sight and hearing of the sublime, the picturesque (pleasing prospects) and the beautiful. The uncanny as an aesthetics of smell is a kind of anti- or counter-aesthetics, especially to the sublime, which disrupts phallocentric sexual difference and its privileging of sight as the smell of the uncanny can be and has been strongly associated with female sexuality (Gallop, 1982, p. 27). The uncanny is associated with smell, but not just with any smell. The smell which evokes the uncanny is what Freud calls 'a very specific smell' which emanates from the virtual crocodiles but is not closely associated with them. This smell which Freud does not name (and hence represses as he does generally with the sense of smell by relegating references to it to what Gallop (1982, p. 28) calls his 'smelly footnotes' (Freud, 1985a, p. 288, n. 1, p. 295, n. 3) could be associated, given the lack of a discriminating aesthetics of smell, in the patriarchal mind, or to its nose, with the odour of female genitalia, which for Freud were the ultimate *unheimlich*, the (un)homely or uncanny.

This uncanny odour is, however, not the passive reverse of the sublime sight, but its active obverse, a kind of anti- or de-sublimation. The odour of female genitalia, the '*odour di femina*,' Gallop (1982, p. 27) argues, 'becomes odious, nauseous, because it threatens to undo the achievements of repression and sublimation, threatens to return the subject to the powerlessness, intensity and anxiety of an immediate, unmediated connection with the body of the mother,' and with 'Mother Earth,' I would add, and with those regions with similarly offensive odours to the patriarchal nose, such as swamps.

The uncanny smell of the wetland entails a return *to* the repressed, as do uncanny smells in general (see Figure 1.1, p. 4). This return is associated by Freud with the artefacts of colonialism which bear the traces of other, alien or exotic places and peoples. Freud construes this return to the repressed as leading back to an old, animistic conception of the universe (Freud, 1985b, p. 363). These animistic stages leave traces which, for Freud, manifest themselves and are expressed in the uncanny. In other words, in the uncanny the traces left by the 'animistic stages,' or more precisely in this context, left by destruction of wetlands, are retraced.

No space, Henri Lefebvre (1991, p. 164; see also pp. 212, 403) argues, 'ever vanishes utterly, leaving no traces.' Filled or drained wetlands have not vanished entirely leaving no traces. For Lefebvre (1991, p. 37), like Freud, 'the past leaves its traces,' yet for Lefebvre, unlike Freud, places also leave their traces. The uncanny could be seen to be the obverse of the Freudian symptom (and as discussed in chapter 4). Unlike the symptom which, for Freud (1973, pp. 296–312), leaves traces of the unconscious on the surface of the body of the patient, the uncanny reworks the traces and returns the subject momentarily to the unconscious and to the surfaces of the body (see Figure 1.1, p. 4) which have been inscribed, and some of whose depths have been invested, by capitalism.

The distinction between trace and inscription is crucial for psychoanalytic ecology. Trace and inscription are not two sorts of writing, but writing is double, or split between the desire to perform and to leave only traces, and the drive to inscribe and to leave durable, if not permanent, marks, to erect monuments. The body is a site of performance of traces and a surface of inscription where the body is not only the human body but also the body of the earth. The crucial distinction for understanding cultural difference is not between orality and (alphabetic) literacy as all cultures have writing and all cultures are literate in reading signs and making meaning from the signs they produce. Rather the crucial distinction is between the trace and the inscription, between traditional, matrifocal cultures and patriarchal (including modern) ones; between cultures of first, or worked, nature and cultures of second, or worked over (even overworked) nature – and not between nature and culture (see Giblett, 2011, chapter 1 for the cultures of natures).

The fundamental civil engineering event of the modern age and the modern culture of nature is the draining and filling of wetlands for dry land agriculture, as it was for the establishment of the ancient city and the sublime modern city (see Giblett, 2016). The fundamental land ownership event is the enclosure of commons (land owned in common) into private property, 'a plain enough case of class robbery' as E. P. Thompson (1968, p. 237) puts it. These two foundational events of modernity coincide with the enclosure and drainage of the Fens and other wetlands as documented by the historical geographer and economic historian H. C. Darby (1956, 1974, 1983). Enclosure of the commons into private property is to the beautiful as drainage is to sublimation. Both enclosure and drainage were exercised against the slimy. For Freud (1964, p. 80) the culture-work of his famous and oft-quoted pronouncement of 'where id was, there ego shall be' is, in the terms of his less-quoted analogy, 'not unlike the draining of the Zuider Zee.' The draining of the Zuider Zee was probably the single largest drainage project ever undertaken, amounting to over half a million acres (van Veen, 1949, p. 52). The devastating effects of this project on the local people, their bioregion and livelihood are graphically depicted in the film *Doodwaater*, literally 'dead water.'

Dyking the Zuider Zee produced dead water and no doubt the draining of the id produces the dead water of the dammed, and damned, wetland of the bourgeois ego unlike the living black water of the wild wetlands of indigenous cultures. Yet for Freud (1964, p. 73) the id needs to be drained because it is 'a chaos, a cauldron full of seething excitations' which run into it from the instincts. If culture-work is ultimately draining instinct, then the threat of instinct for Freud (1973, p. 353) is that it 'would break down every dam and wash away the laboriously erected work of civilisation' and we would flounder about, as Jean François Lyotard (1993, p. 58, 1989, p. 15) puts it, in the swamp of uncertainty that fashions the instincts themselves.

Psychogeopathology

The uncanny is applicable not only to the b(l)ack waters of the swamp, but also to the dark underworld of the city which for Freud was an object, or more precisely abject, of horror and fascination. The uncanny for Freud is a feeling or state of fascination and horror evoked by the 'dark continent,' whether it be of Africa, female sexuality, the slums, the swamp, or its monstrous creatures, such as alligators or crocodiles. The city itself manifests symptoms of its own repressed, principally the wetlands on which it was built, and of its own psychogeopathology to fill or drain wetlands. Symptoms of psychopathology for Freud were inscribed on the surface of the patient's body in the form of his or her behaviour. Symptoms of psychogeopathology are inscribed on the surface of the body of the earth in the form of the city and its behaviour. Chapter 4 of *Psychoanalytic Ecology* considers the city as symptom and Freud's uncanny walk in the red-light district of an Italian town.

Psychogeopathology has had a direct and devastating impact not only on wetlands and the city, but also on the land more generally in resource extraction industries, such as mining (the basis for manufacturing) and pastoralism (the pastoral industry, industrialized sheep and cattle grazing, not small-scale sustainable herding). The proponents of both industries often figure them as orally and anally sadistic in consuming good things and excreting bad ones. In psychoanalytic terms, oral and anal sadism are psychopathologies in which oral and anal desires and fears of an alimental and excremental (eating and excreting) nature are played out: the desire to consume good things; the desire for fairness and symmetry in an exchange of good things; the desire to get rid of bad things; the fear of being consumed; and the fear of fairness and symmetry being exercised back against one in an exchange of bad things.

These desires and fears are enacted in both the mining and pastoral industries as they consume greedily and gluttonously the good things of the generous earth, excrete ungratefully their bad wastes into it, and then expect the earth to hide them – hardly an equitable exchange! Mining employs monstrous machines to devour the earth and defecate on it, as does pastoralism with domesticated animals. As industrial mining and pastoralism exercise oral and anal sadism against the earth, they are psycho*geo*pathologies. Psychopathological symptoms are manifested in association with what could be called 'wetland pathology,' but also with what Leopold (1991, pp. 212–217) called in general 'land pathology' in 'the collective organism of land and society.' Psychogeopathology is the psychological counterpart of land- or geo-pathology. Both always operate together hence 'psychogeopathology.'

Industrial mining and pastoralism are two cases in point of psychogeopathology. Chapters 5 and 6 of *Psychoanalytic Ecology* psychoanalyse these investments of desire and capital, yields of pleasure and profit, and relations of power and work in the mining and pastoral industries by drawing on both Klein's and Abraham's to analyse the psychogeopathologies of oral and anal sadism. Neo-Freudian psychoanalysis is also invoked in the final chapter of *Psychoanalytic Ecology* to call for psycho-symbiosis with the earth by drawing on both Mahler's and Jessica Benjamin's work on psychological symbiosis to promote environ-mental health. Psychoanalytic ecology and participatory postmodern ecology work together to address the personal, political, corporeal, cultural and historical dimensions – the psychodynamics, economics, semiotics and symbiotics – of humans' relationship with the living earth at the local, regional and global levels and at the micro- and macro-scales (for participatory postmodern ecology, see Giblett, 2011, especially pp. 50–55).

Psychoanalysis arose in the heyday of industrial capitalism and bears the marks of its patriarchal parentage. It diagnosed and attempted to cure psychopathological symptoms manifested in individuals. It was both a product of patriarchal capitalist culture and a palliative for it at the individual and cultural levels, in the private and public spheres. It neglected, or even repressed, the biosphere and other -ospheres (see Giblett, 2011, chapter 2) and the underlying cultural, historical and ecological causes of psychopathology diagnosed in *Psychoanalytic Ecology*. It also had little to say about technology and its relation to psychopathology and psychogeopathology. Freudian psychoanalysis addressed the role of technology in psychopathology, most famously in the Fort/Da game with its attempt to master absence and lack, but nothing to say about the role of technology in the psychogeopathology of orally and anally sadistic and monstrous machines and their drive for mastery of nature.

Although psychoanalysis arose in the heyday of industrial capitalism and is the son of its patriarchal father, it can be used to analyse and engage in a talking cure of its psychogeopathologies just as it did with its psychopathologies. The limited success of the latter can partially be ascribed to its locating the causes of symptoms within the claustrophobic and sequestered confines of the domestic private sphere of the patriarchal conjugal family rather than in the larger private sphere of civil society, the public sphere of the nation-state and their interactions with the bio- and other -ospheres. Psychoanalytic ecology addresses these larger interactions and their psychogeopathologies. The drive here is not only to diagnose the symptoms of psychogeopathology and to engage in a talking cure of them and their causes but also to prevent their manifestation in the first place by promoting environ-mental health through mutuality and sacrality (as discussed in the final chapter of *Psychoanalytic Ecology*).

References

Brown, N. 1959. *Life Against Death: The Psychoanalytical Meaning of History*. Hanover, NH: Wesleyan University Press.

Bunyan, J. 2008. *The Pilgrim's Progress*, R. Pooley, ed. London: Penguin.

Darby, H. C. 1956. *The Draining of the Fens*, second edition. Cambridge: Cambridge University Press.

Darby, H. C. 1974. *The Medieval Fenland*, second edition. Newton Abbot: David and Charles.

Darby, H. C. 1983. *The Changing Fenland*. Cambridge: Cambridge University Press.

Freud, S. 1919. The 'Uncanny'. *In: The Standard Edition of the Complete Psychological Works of Sigmund Freud, Volume XVII (1917–1919): An Infantile Neurosis and Other Works*. London: Hogarth, pp. 217–256.

Freud, S. 1964. *New Introductory Lectures on Psycho-Analysis. The Standard Edition of the Complete Psychological Works of Sigmund Freud, Volume XXII (1932–1936)*. London: Hogarth.

Freud, S. 1973. *Introductory Lectures on Psychoanalysis*, Penguin Freud Library 1. Harmondsworth: Penguin.

Freud, S. 1975. Findings, Ideas, Problems. *In: The Standard Edition of the Complete Psychological Works of Sigmund Freud, Volume XXIII*. London: Hogarth, pp. 299–300.

Freud, S. 1985a. *Civilization, Society and Religion*, Penguin Freud Library 12. Harmondsworth: Penguin.

Freud, S. 1985b. The 'Uncanny'. *In: Art and Literature*, Penguin Freud Library 14. Harmondsworth: Penguin, pp. 335–376.

Freud, S. 2003. *The Uncanny*, D. Mclintock, trans. London: Penguin.

Freud, S. 2005. *On Murder, Mourning and Melancholia*, S. Whiteside, trans. London: Penguin.

Gallop, J. 1982. *Feminism and Psychoanalysis: The Daughter's Seduction*. London: Palgrave Macmillan.

Giblett, R. 1996. *Postmodern Wetlands: Culture, History, Ecology*. Edinburgh: Edinburgh University Press.

Giblett, R. 2011. *People and Places of Nature and Culture*. Bristol: Intellect Books.

Giblett, R. 2016. *Cities and Wetlands: The Return of the Repressed in Nature and Culture*. London: Bloomsbury.

Giblett, R. 2018. *Environmental Humanities and Theologies: Ecoculture, Literature and the Bible*. London: Routledge.

Hoffman, E. 1982. The Sandman. *In:* R. Hollingdale, trans., *Tales*, London: Penguin, pp. 85–125.

Kant, I. 1960. *Observations on the Feeling of the Beautiful and Sublime*, J. Goldth-wait, trans. Berkeley: University of California Press.

Laplanche, J. and J-B. Pontalis 1973. Sublimation. *In:* D. Nicholson-Smith, trans., *The Language of Psychoanalysis*. London: Hogarth, pp. 431–434.

Lefebvre, H. 1991. *The Production of Space*, D. Nicholson-Smith, trans. Oxford: Blackwell.

Leopold, A. 1949. *A Sand County Almanac and Sketches Here and There*. New York: Oxford University Press.

Leopold, A. 1991. Land Pathology. *In:* S. Flader and J. Callicott, eds., *The River of the Mother of God and Other Essays*. Madison: University of Wisconsin Press, pp. 212–217.

Leopold, A. 1999. The Land-Health Concept and Conservation. *In:* J. Baird Cal-licott and E. Freyfogle, eds., *For the Health of the Land: Previously Unpublished Essays and Other Writings*. Washington, DC: Island Press/Covelo, CA: Shearwa-ter Books, pp. 218–226.

Lyotard, J. 1989. *Lyotard Reader*, A. Benjamin, ed. Oxford: Blackwell.

Lyotard, J. 1993. *Libidinal Economy*, I. Hamilton Grant, trans. London: Athlone.

Paglia, C. 1991. *Sexual Personae: Art and Decadence from Nefertiti to Emily Dick-inson*. New York: Vintage.

Ramsar Convention Bureau. *The Importance of Wetlands*. Accessed online: www.ramsar.org/about/the-importance-of-wetlands

Randolph, J. 2001a. Looking Back at Cyborgs. *In:* B. Grenville, ed., *The Uncanny: Experiments in Cyborg Culture*. Vancouver: Arsenal Pulp Press, pp. 182–186.

Randolph, J. 2001b. Transgressed Boundaries: Potent Fusions and Dangerous Pos-sibilities. *In:* B. Grenville, ed., *The Uncanny: Experiments in Cyborg Culture*. Vancouver: Arsenal Pulp Press, pp. 95–99.

Simmel, G. 1950. The Metropolis and Mental Life. *In:* K. Wolff, trans., *The Sociol-ogy of Georg Simmel*. New York: Palgrave Macmillan, pp. 409–424.

Sofoulis, Z. 1988. *Through the Lumen: Frankenstein and the Optics of Re-Origination*, Ph.D. Thesis. History of Consciousness, University of California, Santa Cruz.

Spengler, O. 1932. *The Decline of the West,* C. Atkinson, trans. London: George Allen and Unwin.

Thompson, E. 1968. *The Making of the English Working Class*. Harmondsworth: Penguin.

Tremayne, P. 1985. *Swamp*. New York: St Martin's Press.

Van Veen, J. 1949. *Dredge Drain Reclaim: The Art of a Nation*. The Hague: Trio.

2 Mourning, melancholy and marshes

Wetlands were once thought to be bad for the body under the miasmatic theory of disease that malaria, literally 'bad air,' could be caught be breathing miasma or bad air. Wetlands could also be bad for the mind. Indeed, they can plunge the mind into melancholia, and even into madness. In a typical assessment made more than one hundred years ago the later-to-be president of the United States Theodore Roosevelt (cited by Brooks, 2014, p. 111) referred to 'the melancholy marshes' in the 'lonely lands' of 'the wilderness.' More specifically, the corpse beneath the swamp is not only a reminder of death, but also a vector of melancholy. Such sentiments were voiced when Hubert Davis (1962, p. 21) referred to 'the stench of a rotting carcass of some depraved hunter lost in the depths of its [the Great Dismal Swamp's] melancholy jungles.'

This assessment of the marsh as melancholic can also be found in the work of those masters of dejection, the Romantic poets. Percy Bysshe Shelley (1975, pp. 51–52), for example, referred to 'a wide and melancholy waste/Of putrid marshes' when evoking 'the Spirit of Solitude.' Previously Samuel Pepys (1972, p. 311) in the late seventeenth century travelled 'over most sad Fenns (all the way observing the sad life that the people of that place . . . do live).' More recently, the map of 'the world' of those 1920s classics of Anglophone children's literature, *Winnie-the-Pooh* and *The House at Pooh Corner*, with its Christopher Robin of the clean and proper body, has that arch manic-depressive donkey Eeyore living in 'Eeyore's Gloomy Place' which is 'rather boggy and sad' (Milne, 1958, frontispiece map). Other examples in adolescent literature are the Swamps of Sadness in Michael Ende's *The Neverending Story* and the Dead Marshes in J. R. R. Tolkien's *The Lord of the Rings* (see Giblett, 2018, pp. 29–34).

The slough of despond

The most famous depiction in English culture of a depressed place (in two senses) is Bunyan's 'Slough of Despond' in *Pilgrim's Progress*, first published in 1678. Louis Marin (cited by Fritzell, 1978, p. 528) has described *Pilgrim's Progress* as 'the most influential religious book ever composed in the English language.' It is also the second most published book in the English language after the Bible. No doubt part of its pre-eminent influence has been to educate generations of readers that an ecologically functioning wetland is not what it seems, and is, but an allegorical emblem for a sump of iniquity that would drag the unsuspecting and unwary Christian down and entrap him/her for all eternity. Bunyan (2008, p. 18) relates how 'this miry slough is such a place as cannot be mended; it is the descent whither the scum and filth that attends conviction for sin doth continually run, and therefore it is called the Slough of Despond.'

The same figure is used with the same pejorative overtones (though not of course as an allegorical emblem for sin) in Donna Haraway's recent proclamation that 'like Christian in *Pilgrim's Progress* . . . I am committed to skirting the slough of despond and the parasite-infested swamps of nowhere to reach more salubrious environs' (Haraway, 1992, p. 295; see p. 329, n. 1 for her exclusion of the allegory of sin as slough of despond in invoking *Pilgrim's Progress*). One wonders salubrious for whom? In whose terms? And if the slough of despond is not an allegorical emblem for sin, what is 'sin' in Haraway's theologized, or at least moralized, wetlandscape? What is 'nowhere'? Is it 'the amniotic effluvia of terminal industrialism' that Haraway refers to later (but without making any explicit connection) and that we have encountered earlier? If so, then the figure would have a critical edge and contemporary pertinence; if not, then Haraway's use of the figure would seem to be gratuitously uncritical about the use of tropes and blind to the politics of place (place-blind and even misaquaterrist).

Yet she argues in these very same two pages that 'nature is . . . a *topos*, a place,' that 'nature is also *trópos*, a trope' and later for a 'politics of articulation' which speaks with an intersubject rather than for 'a politics of representation' which speaks for and on behalf of an object (Haraway, 1992, pp. 296, 311–313). But as nature is also place*s*, *topoi*, as different *topoi* are troped in different ways with some being valorized at the expense or to the detriment of others, so there is a politics of the articulation of tropes of topes, a politics of *trópoi* of *topoi*, not least of wetlands. Haraway cares about 'the survival of jaguars and the chimpanzee, and the Hawaiian land snails, and the spotted owl, and a lot of other earth*lings*' (Haraway, 1992 p. 311; my emphasis), but does she care about the survival of sloughs (of despond), (parasite-infested) swamps and uncharismatic micro-fauna (like parasites)?

No such qualms of conscience or ethical dilemmas were to trouble English writers after Bunyan despite the increasing secularization of English culture. The slough of despond was divested of its religious overtones, but not of its pejorative, misaquaterrist associations. Instead of being

a place of evil construed in religious terms, it became a place of melancholia, a kind of secular despondency or despair. Dickens, for example, has 'the
Slough of Despond' in *Hard Times*, as well as 'the slough of inanity.' 'The
social swamp' as Thomas Huxley (1989, p. 335) called *'la misère'* in 1888
could be 'a Slough of Despond.' Dickens saves his most scathing attack on
the swamp as a slough of despond for chapter 23 of *Martin Chuzzlewit* (see
Giblett, 2018, pp. 101–103).

The slough of despond, rather than being rehabilitated or its pejorative
connotations reversed in the process of increasing secularization, came to
stand for the dark side of the Enlightenment and Romanticism despite their
differences. The Slough of Despond, Peter Fritzell has argued:

> is the well-remembered antithesis to enlightenment and romantic
> thought. . . . With the declaration of man's [*sic*] perfectibility and the
> affirmation of sublime and picturesque vistas, with the denial of man's
> imperfectibility and the negation of landscapes which do not fit the
> conventions of the sublime or the picturesque people of the nineteenth
> century can proceed to their new-found manifest destiny. They can
> proceed with the story of exploitation, the story of draining, ditching,
> clearing and filling, which will improve, civilise, humanise, and finally
> redeem the nonhuman environment.
>
> (Fritzell, 1978, p. 529)

Such a place as the slough of despond as the antithesis of enlightenment
would seem to make the ideal setting or backdrop for the private detective
story as it is a place of almost impenetrable evil and darkness which can
only be pierced by the penetrating light of reason brought to bear upon it by
the superior intellect and insight of the great man himself (for it is invariably a man so why not a feminist detective story which inverts, or better still
subverts, this scenario?). It is hardly surprising then that the most famous
private detective of them all in probably his most famous story of all should
have to deal with a slough of despond. This is, of course, Sherlock Holmes
in *The Hound of the Baskervilles* with its Great Grimpen Mire (see Giblett,
2018, pp. 105–106).

Similarly, Fergus Hume in his even better-selling detective novel than *The
Hound* and 'the first popular Melbourne novel,' according to John Arnold
(1983, pp. 7–8), *The Mystery of a Hansom Cab*, first published in 1886,
evokes vividly the Dantesque 'Infernal Regions' 'off Little Bourke St.' Like
the epic hero descending into the underworld to slay monsters and return
home triumphant, 'the detective led the way down a dark lane, which felt
like a furnace owing to the heat of the night' (Hume, 1999, pp. 178–179).
The infernal distress of the slums of Bourke Street can be contrasted with

what Marjorie Clark (in Arnold, 1983, p. 69) in 1927 described as 'the cool charm of its [Collins Street's] arcades.' Worse for the detective entering the slums of Bourke Street, 'it was like walking in the valley of the shadow of death [. . .] And, indeed, it was not unlike the description in Bunyan's famous allegory what with the semidarkness, the wild lights and shadows' (Hume, 1999, p. 180). Hume combines Dante and Bunyan (and the biblical Psalmist, as Bunyan is drawing on *Psalm* 23) in an omnibus and ominous grab bag of tropes for the urban underworld.

As an aside here, these pages are excerpted and reproduced as a quintes-sential depiction of the 'mean streets and back alleys' of late nineteenth-century Melbourne as depicted in crime fiction for the anthology *Literary Melbourne* edited by Stephen Grimwade (2009, pp. 187–190). The refer-ence to 'the valley of the shadow of death' is later misquoted as 'the shadow of the valley of death' (Grimwade, 2009, p. 244). This misquotation gives a new nuance to the idea of death valley transposed here from the remote deserts of California to inner-city Melbourne. Both are hot and deadly places. As Michael Cannon (1976, pp. 42–43) puts it, 'the Angel of Death came early and stayed late in the Melbourne of 1892 and 1893' with 'epi-demics of influenza, typhoid and measles [. . .] which [. . .] killed thou-sands.' It is only a hop, skip and a jump from Bunyan's and the Psalmist's 'valley of the shadow of death' to Hume's alley of the shadow of death and Grimwade's shadow of the valley of death.

The detective's journey into the urban underworld is not only physical but also moral and allegorical. The detective novel is a secular allegory of literal and spiritual descent and ascent, of degradation and salvation, just like the sacred allegory of Bunyan's *Pilgrims Progress*. In the case of Sherlock Hol-mes, the detective's journey also includes a descent into the Bunyanesque 'Slough of Despond' of Great Grimpen Mire in *The Hound of the Baskervilles* (as we have already seen). Similarly, Flinders Street in 1845 was described as 'that slough of despond' (cited by Annear, 2014, p. 40). The swamp outside the city in the country, or inside the city in the muddy streets or slums, is a secularized satanic space. Perhaps it is fitting that the *flâneur* is a creature of the arcades, which Johann Geist (1983, p. vii) describes in his monumental history of the arcade as 'a secularised sacred space.' The swamp is a secular-ized satanic space for the detective that is a sacred space and place for indig-enous, traditional peoples. The secularized satanic space of the swamp could be the native or natural swamp in the country, or the feral or cultural 'swamp' of the slums in the city in which the latter is used as a figure for the latter.

In *Pilgrim's Progress* Bunyan (2008, p. 65) takes the fourth verse of *Psalm* 23 referring to the valley of the shadow of death for his text and sermonizes on how 'Christian must needs go through it, because the way to the Celestial City lay through the midst of it. ' Typically the detective in the modern city must go through the valley of the shadow of death of the underworld of the slums in order to protect the upper city of the upper ten thousand living in the upper world of the crystalline celestial city. Or the hero of the modern epic of the novel, such as Jean Valjean in Hugo's *Les Miserables*, must descend into the underworld of the sewers of Paris (see Giblett, 2016, chapter 3). The modern hero of the tourist can even follow in Valjean's footsteps and go on a tour of the sewers of Paris in the marshy underworld of 'Lutetia,' the Latin-cum-Celtic name for the 'filthy marsh' in which the city was founded. Although Melbourne as the 'Paris of the South' does not have such an official tour of its sewers, 'a small group has for several decades mounted regular unlawful explorations of Melbourne's stormwater drains and tunnels' in what Kristin Otto (2005, p. 175) calls 'a Yarra [River] underworld.' Sophie Cunningham (2011, p. 147) also comments that 'while Melbourne does not boast Paris's hundreds of kilometres of underground tunnels, it does have Anzac, a cavernous drain under South Yarra where many parties have been held over the years.'

Later in *Pilgrim's Progress* Christian is informed that 'the valley [of the shadow of death] itself' is:

> as dark as pitch: we also saw there the hobgoblins, satyrs, and dragons of the pit; we heard also in that valley a continual howling and yelling, as of a people under unutterable misery, who there sat bound in affliction and irons; and over that hung the discouraging clouds of confusion; Death also does always spread his wings over it. In a word, it is every whit dreadful, being utterly without order.
>
> (Bunyan, 2008, pp. 67, 69)

As the underworld is a monstrous place itself inhabited by monsters, such as dragons, so is 'the monster city.' In similar vein, Little Bourke Street in *The Mystery of a Hansom Cab* has its 'weird and grotesquely horrible' inhabitants (Hume, 1999, p. 220). In a word, they are monstrous. Little Bourke Street contrasts with Bourke Street proper, not only in the type of inhabitants, but also in the mode of illumination. Bourke Street is described 'as the brilliantly lit street' produced by 'electric lights,' which highlight the members of the crowd caught in 'the full glare of the electric light.' By contrast, Little Bourke Street is lit by 'sparsely scattered gas lamps' with their 'dim light,' whereas the lanes have no lights or lamps so they are dark, or:

> not quite dark, for the atmosphere had that luminous kind of haze so observable in Australian twilights, and the weird light was just sufficient to make the darkness visible.
>
> (Hume, 1999, pp. 178–180)

Typically the fictive detective of the modern city enlightens the benighted, brings light to darkness and illuminates the crepuscular gloom of crime and grime.

In her biographical and critical study of Hume's novel, Lucy Sussex (2015, p. 7) argues that it had 'an important role in establishing detective fiction as a publishing category' as he is 'one of the most influential crime writers of all time' who wrote 'the biggest-selling crime novel of the nineteenth century, and one of the most important Australian books ever.' Sussex traces the etymology of the word 'detective' and how it literally means 'de-roofing' as 'a detective raises the roof, figuratively.' The detective in the detective story, and the detective storyteller, raises the roof of dwelling spaces, looks inside and reveals what is inside to the reader. The detective and detective story reader are positioned as snooping voyeurs.

Sussex (2015, pp. 9–10) also traces how this uncovering and de-roofing had a demonic function and cites Dickens in *Dombey and Son* published in 1848 who pleaded for 'a good spirit who would take the house-tops off.' David Grann (2017, p. 57) similarly traces how 'the term "to detect" derived from the Latin verb to "unroof," and because the devil, according to legend, allowed his henchmen to peer voyeuristically into houses by removing their roofs, detectives were known as "the devil's disciples".' In the Sherlock Holmes' story 'A Case of Identity,' Conan Doyle has Holmes describe the detective's work of unroofing in similar terms (albeit without the etymology and the theological overtones). The detective in the detective story, and the detective storyteller too, perform these socially useful, but morally ambiguous, roles of the good, or demonic, spirit. Both were *flâneurs* who entered 'the city's central hell [of] the slums,' as Sussex (2015, p. 60) puts it in relation to Hume and *Hansom Cab*. As with the circles of Dante's hell, or inferno, the city has a centre, and its centre is the lower depth of its slums and sewers, the grotesque lower urban strata. The seemingly most secularized literary genre of the detective story about the modern city has strong theological undertones.

Melancholy

Despondency is another name for melancholy that is the immanent counterpart to the transcendental sublime and the spiritual counterpart to the psychological uncanny. As the uncanny is a secular theology for a world in which God is dead, so melancholy is a secular spirituality in the lower psychopathological register of the abject. In 1933 Gershom Scholem (Benjamin and Scholem, 1992, p. 81) included a poem in a letter to Walter Benjamin the last line of which concludes that 'where God once stood now stands: Melancholy.' Melancholy is the abject spirituality of a world in which God is dead and, as Terry Eagleton (1986, p. 41) argues, 'the appropriate neurosis for a profit-based society' driven by greed for, and indulging in gluttony of, the earth's resources. Just as the aesthetic and philosophical sublime lifts one up to the heady heights of intellection and theory close to the divine, so the psychological and spiritual melancholy of the uncanny depresses one down into the grotesque lower bodily and earthly strata of slime close to the demonic beneath the black sun of melancholia (see Figure 1.1, p. 4 and Giblett, 1996, chapters 2 and 7).

Melancholy is associated with death, or at least with the valley of the shadow of death (the precursor to death) and with mourning (the aftermath of death). Melancholia and mourning are similar for Freud. In his 1917 essay, 'Mourning and Melancholia,' Freud argued that mourning is 'commonly the reaction to the loss of a beloved person,' whereas melancholia 'may be a reaction to the loss of a beloved object' (Freud, 2005, pp. 203, 205). The loved object which is lost for the melancholic is specifically the breast of the mother and the water which is breast milk or the water of the wetland, the first water which nourished life (on earth), the breast of Mother Earth.

More broadly, the loved and lost object can be 'nature' generally as Freud (2005, pp. 195–200) identified and discussed in his essay 'On Transience' published in 1916, the year before 'Mourning and Melancholia.' For Freud (2005, p. 199), mourning and melancholia were particularly acute during the destruction of World War I that 'robbed the world of its beauties' and 'destroyed [. . .] the beauty of its landscapes.' Freud (2005, p. 198) found some consolation in the cycle of the seasons in which 'the beauty of nature [. . .] returns the following year after the ravages of winter' and in the fact that 'that return may be seen as eternal in terms of the length of our lives.' The melancholic ego, however, is immersed in the moment and does not have the time-scale of the eternal. Freud (2005, p. 197) describes a young poet who demonstrates the affliction of, and fixation on, transience that is the topic of the essay and the impetus for writing it. The young poet values transient objects because of their 'scarcity over time' and so experiences the 'painful world-weariness' of melancholia. By contrast, Freud values enduring objects because of their generosity over time and so experiences the pleasurable world-liveliness of eternality.

Instead of investing desire in the object of love, such as the breast and/or the mother and gaining some return of pleasure on that investment (the economic metaphor is appropriate), the melancholic ego 'wants to incorporate this object into itself, and in accordance with the oral or cannibalistic phase of libidinal development in which it is, it wants to do so by devouring it,' or by simply 'eating it' in the less orally sadistic terms of the more recent translation (Freud, 1984, p. 258, 2005, p. 210). In environmental terms, the melancholic wants to incorporate the nourishing qualities of the living waters of the wetland breast into himself by devouring it through drainage or filling, and even by creating artificial ones. The object of investment was initially an object of love which was later lost.

Freud goes on to distinguish between mourning and melancholia by arguing that 'in mourning it is the world which has becomes poor and empty; in melancholia it is the ego itself' (Freud, 1984, p. 254, 2005, pp. 205–206). In mourning the world is experienced as loss whereas in melancholia the ego is experienced as lost. Freud outlined the process whereby melancholia establishes an 'identification of the ego with the abandoned object' (Freud, 1984, p. 258, 2005, p. 209): 'the shadow of the object fell upon the ego [. . .] as though it were an object, the forsaken [or "abandoned"] object. In this way the loss of the object was transferred into a loss of ego' (Freud, 1984, p. 258, 2005, p. 209). As Mikkel Borch-Jacobson (1989, p. 183) concludes in his discussion of melancholy, 'the ego becomes the object,' or even more succinctly, 'the lost object [is] me' as Nicolas Abraham and Maria Torok (1984) put it, as a way of denying or disavowing the loss of the loved object in narcissistic inversion.[1]

Along similar lines to Freud's discussion of eternality, Walter Benjamin (2003, p. 395) developed the concept of *Jetztzeit*, a theological category of the messianic now coming out of traditional Judeo-Christian theology (with its concept of *Kairos* derived from Greek thought and probably via the Christian apostle and New Testament epistolary writer, St Paul) and combined with Marxist eschatology to indicate a messianic irruption in the present that blasts open the continuum of history (in a word, revolution) and counters melancholia. In a recent discussion of melancholy in relation to Benjamin's work on the German mourning play, Ilit Ferber (2013, p. 20) reiterates along Freudian lines that 'the lost object continues to exist, now as part of the dejected subject.' The lost wetlands destroyed by cities continue to exist, now as part of the dejected subject of the citizen who maintains 'a relationship with an absent lost object' (Ferber, 2013, p. 43), just as the subject maintains a relationship with absent lost wetlands by being oblivious to them or by retelling their stories, by remarking their presence in the past on maps and their absence in the present on maps too. The aim thereby is that 'the relationship between subject and object is overturned' (Ferber, 2013, p. 46). Subject and object become what Julia Kristeva (1982, pp. 1–2) calls (the) abject, or what Nietzsche called the body (see Giblett, 2008, pp. 3–5). The subject and object return to the pre-subject and pre-object phase in which both were abject. The abject precedes the subject and the object. It is the third party that made both possible. The dejected subject in no longer dejected, but abjected and is no longer subject, but abject.

This de-subjectification, de-objectification and abjectification contrasts with what Ferber (2013, p. 59) describes as 'the destructive nature of the melancholic's response to loss' in which 'the melancholic devours his lost love-object in order to retain it; in demonstrating his endless loyalty, he destroys it. Therein lies the paradox: the only way to retain the object is to destroy it.' The melancholic devours his lost love-object of wetlands by using monstrous drainers and dredgers in order to retain them (literally behind retaining walls as in cities such as Venice) and retrain them and their aberrant water (as in the city of Venice in canals; see Giblett, 2016, chapter 5), but in doing so kills the wetland as a living being, as a habitat for other living beings. He kills the thing he loves, rather than loving the thing he kills as indigenous cultures do (see Giblett, 2011, p. 215). For Ferber (2013, p. 73 'the melancholic's lost object is either dead (in the case of human loss) or absent (in the case of a more abstract loss).' In the case of the destruction and loss of a wetland, the melancholic's lost object is both dead (a case of non-human loss) *and* absent (a case of a concrete loss).

Moreover, for Ferber (2013, p. 73), 'in both cases the pathology lies in the subject's inability to recognize the loss and the insistence of maintaining the dead object as "half-alive" within the melancholic consciousness, thus rendering the boundary between life and death indefinite and thus indistinct.' In the case of the destruction and loss of a wetland, the psychogeopathology lies not only within what Ferber outlines, but also within not recognizing the wetland as a place of both life and death in which life and death are mixed, but wherein the boundary between them is definite and thus distinct. The melancholic's half-alive lost object for Ferber (2013, p. 102) is 'what is not yet dead but no longer alive.' This object is buried alive in a tomb when, Ferber (2013, p. 102) goes on to relate, 'the melancholic carves out an internal tomb for his lost object, engendering an internal topography in which the living ego and the dead object coexist,' just as in Venice the city goes on living above its entombed dead lagoons of once living wombs of wetlands (see Giblett, 2016, chapter 5).

In the concrete cases of the subject's relation to non-human living objects, such as animals and wetlands, the living ego and the dead object coexist by the living ego continuing to live by killing the object (see Giblett, 2008, pp. 119–120; Giblett and Tolonen, 2012, p. 41, 45). They are entombed as dead object, but they were once life-giving wombs. Death, as Ferber (2013, p. 104) concludes, 'does not mark the end of life. . .: the two states exist concomitantly,' as they do in the wetland's ecology. Moreover, for Ferber (2013, p. 115) 'the dead are never completely dead, and the past can never be hermetically closed.' The lost wetlands are never completely dead, and the past is still an open book, as it is in Venice (see Giblett, 2016, chapter 5). Venice is the wetland city *par excellence* not only in terms of its past and its history as a city founded in a swamp, but also in the present and its current culture as a rich source of metaphor and of psychological travail in which the metaphors are symptomatic of its mournful and melancholic psychogeopathology.

Melancholy in association with the city of Venice is played out in Vera Brittain's autobiographical study, *Testament of Youth*. As she 'glides smoothly' in a gondola 'over the rippling grey silk of the Grand Canal' on her post-World War I tour of Europe, the view of Venice for Brittain (1978, p. 479) is tinged with melancholy and mourning as she associates the Venetian waters with the death of her fiancé in France and brother in Italy during the War. The Grand Canal is associated not only with melancholy and mourning but also with magic as Brittain 'with melancholy possessiveness . . . looked upon those enchanted waters . . . those fairy lagoons, incredible as a gorgeous mirage in the muffled silence.' These are the benign waters of the patriarchal Mother Earth. She imagines that her brother 'had died saving this beauty from the fate of Ypres,' in other words, saving the beauty of the city of Venice from the horror of trench warfare, in particular its mud.

Brittain read about the mud of trench warfare in the letters of her brother and fiancé wrote to her and had immediate experience of it as a nurse in France and in the aftermath of the death of her fiancé. In one of his letters from the trenches Brittain's fiancé related that they were 'very wet and muddy. . . . The whole of one's world, at least one's visible and palpable world, is mud in various stages of solidity or stickiness' (Brittain, 1978, p. 206). Mud mixes the elements earth and water, whereas cities and roads separate them as a rule, or should do. Brittain (1978, p. 337) experienced the mud first-hand when she arrives on the Western front and found that 'the roads were liquid with such mud as only wartime France could produce after a few days of rain.' The solidity of earth was liquefied into mud.

The mud of trench warfare, especially its smell, in associated for Brittain with death when she goes through the 'kit' of her fiancé following his death. She wrote to her brother that everything was 'simply caked with mud' and she felt 'overwhelmed by the horror of war' as

> the smell of those clothes was the smell of graveyards and the Dead. The mud of France which covered them was not ordinary mud; it had not the usual clean pure smell of earth, but it was as though it were saturated with dead bodies – dead that had been dead a long, long time.
> (Brittain, 1978, p. 225)

The mud of trench warfare had the smell of death in which earth, water and dead bodies (and shit, though she does not mention this) were mixed. It did have not the usual smell of mud in which earth and water were mixed. Brittain distinguishes the clean, pure smell of earth from the horrific, dirty smell of the mud of trench warfare.

Like most writers about World War I (see Giblett, 2009, chapter 4), Brittain (1978, p. 355) associates the mud of trench warfare with swamps and marshes, such as when she describes how 'the terrific gales and whipping rains of late autumn . . . turned the shell-gashed flats of Flanders into an ocean of marshy mud that made death by drowning almost as difficult to avoid as death from gun-fire.' Yet the wetlandscape of trench warfare is an artificial marsh made by modern industrial warfare, not a native marsh made by hydrogeological processes and ancestral hands.

The wetlandscape of trench warfare is also melancholic for Brittain (1978, p. 356), such as when she describes how 'the Flanders offensive was subsiding dismally into the mud' and refers to 'melancholy Flanders' on the next page. Brittain experiences mourning and melancholia during and after World War I, yet she also experiences these affects in Venice after the war in combination with the magic of the maternal waters of the wetlands – perhaps hardly surprising given her strong feminist beliefs, though she is unable to distinguish the canalized waters of the patriarchal city from the matrifocal waters of the wetlands that preceded the city and which the city destroyed. Although she distinguishes the dirty impure smell of trench warfare from the clean pure smell of earth, she does not regard the former as the product of patriarchal and industrial trench warfare and the latter as the progeny of maternal marshes, nor does she distinguish the artificial 'manmade' marshes of modern industrial warfare from the native marshes made by hydrogeological processes and ancestral hands.

Instead of seeing the object (the breast, the wetland) as lost, the melancholic ego sees itself as lost in a massive act of narcissistic disavowal and egotism. As a result, the ego desires itself, or in the terms of Gilles Deleuze and Felix Guattari (1977, p. 26) 'it is the subject . . . that is missing in desire, or desire that lacks a fixed subject; there is no fixed subject unless there is repression.' Repression is to subjectivity as drainage is to wetlands; repression (and drainage) fix the flows of embodied subjects (and wetlands). Repression is constitutive precisely of *melancholic* subjectivity; subjectivity is melancholic and mournful. The subject desires itself as a product of a melancholic loss of the loved object of the mother and Mother Earth, of the mother's breasts and Mother Earth's breasts, the living waters of wetlands.

As wetlands are increasingly lost from the world and are lost as an object of love which nourishes life, both mourning and melancholia are experienced and exercised in relation to them. The world should be in mourning for the loss of its wetlands which gave it life and nourished it, but instead of being in mourning and regarding the world as losing its wetlands becoming empty or 'bereft' of them, in Gerard Manley Hopkins's (1953, p. 51) apt word, it experiences this loss as a melancholic loss of its own ego, its own selfhood and sense of identity. Selfhood and identity is constituted in relation to something outside itself against which it stands in contradistinction. When that object is lost, as when wetlands are lost, that loss is experienced in melancholia as a loss of the subject. The world is becoming empty of wetlands; the world is losing its wetlands. In patriarchy (the rule of the fathers) and filiarchy (the rule of the sons) wetlands are the bad breast of the world in which, in Klein's terms, the infantile sons try to hide their excrements, but in these psycho-ecological terms they are the womb and breast of the world, the organs of receptivity and bounty as Klein puts it – they are living waters.

Note

1 Renee Aron Lertzman (2013, pp. 124–126) in her discussion of mourning and melancholia in Freud's essay 'On Transience' (and not in his essay on the topic) considers 'the lost or damaged object,' such as 'a body of water,' as outside and separate from the subject, and not as (part of) the subject. Lertzman (2015, p. 117) also invokes 'Freudian melancholia' in her book-length study of environmental melancholia, but does not discuss Freud's essay on mourning and melancholia which seems like a lost opportunity to engage with their psychoanalytic dimensions and to relate them to environmental issues and concerns.

References

Abraham, N. and M. Torok. 1984. A Poetics of Psychoanalysis: 'The Lost Object – Me'. *Substance*, 43, pp. 3–18.

Annear, R. 2014. *Bearbrass: Imagining Early Melbourne*. Melbourne: Black Inc.

Arnold, J. 1983. *The Imagined City: Melbourne in the Mind of Its Writers*. North Sydney: George Allen and Unwin.

Benjamin, W. 2003. *Selected Writings: Volume 4, 1938–1940* H. Eiland and M. Jennings, eds, trans. E. Jephcott and others. Cambridge, MA: The Belknap Press of Harvard University Press.

Benjamin, W. and G. Scholem. 1992. *The Correspondence of Walter Benjamin and Gershom Scholem, 1932–1940*. G. Scholem, ed., G. Smith and A. Lefevre, trans. Cambridge, MA: Harvard University Press.

Borch-Jacobson, M. 1989. *The Freudian Subject*, C. Porter, trans. London: Palgrave Macmillan.

Brittain, V. 1978. *Testament of Youth: An Autobiographical Study of the Years 1900–1925*. London: Virago.

Brooks, P. 2014. *Speaking for Nature: The Literary Naturalists from Transcendentalism to the Birth of the American Environmental Movement*. Mineola, NY: Dover.

Bunyan, J. 2008. *The Pilgrim's Progress*, R. Pooley, ed. London: Penguin.

Cannon, M. 1976. *The Land Boomers*, new illustrated edition. Melbourne: Thomas Nelson.

Cunningham, S. 2011. *Melbourne*. Sydney: New South.

Davis, H. 1962. *The Great Dismal Swamp: Its History, Folklore and Science*, revised edition. Self-published.

Deleuze, G. and F. Guattari. 1977. *Anti-Oedipus: Capitalism and Schizophrenia*, R. Hurley, M. Seem and H. Lane, trans. New York: Viking Press.

Eagleton, T. 1986. *William Shakespeare*. Oxford: Basil Blackwell.

Ferber, I. 2013. *Philosophy and Melancholy: Benjamin's Early Reflections on Theater and Language*. Stanford: Stanford University Press.

Freud, S. 1984. *On Metapsychology: The Theory of Psychoanalysis*, Pelican Freud Library 11. Harmondsworth: Penguin.

Freud, S. 2005. *On Murder, Mourning and Melancholia*, S. Whiteside, trans. London: Penguin.

Fritzell, P. 1978. American Wetlands as Cultural Symbol: Places of Wetlands in American Culture. *In*: P. Greeson, J. Clark and J. Clark, eds., *Wetland Functions and Values: The State of Our Understanding*. Minneapolis: American Water Resources Association, pp. 523–534.

Geist, J. 1983. *Arcades: The History of a Building Type*. Cambridge, MA: The MIT Press.

Giblett, R. 1996. *Postmodern Wetlands: Culture, History, Ecology.* Edinburgh: Edinburgh University Press.

Giblett, R. 2008. *The Body of Nature and Culture*. Basingstoke: Palgrave Macmillan.

Giblett, R. 2009. *Landscapes of Culture and Nature*. Basingstoke: Palgrave Macmillan.

Giblett, R. 2011. *People and Places of Nature and Culture*. Bristol: Intellect Books.

Giblett, R. 2016. *Cities and Wetlands: The Return of the Repressed in Nature and Culture*. London: Bloomsbury.

Giblett, R. 2018. *Environmental Humanities and Theologies: Ecoculture, Literature and the Bible*. London: Routledge.

Giblett, R. and J. Tolonen. 2012. *Photography and Landscape*. Bristol: Intellect Books.

Grann, D. 2017. *Killers of the Flower Moon: Oil, Money, Murder and the Birth of the FBI*. London: Simon and Schuster.

Grimwade, S., ed. 2009. *Literary Melbourne: A Celebration of Writing and Ideas*. Prahran: Hardie Grant.

Haraway, D. 1992. The Promises of Monsters: A Regenerative Politics for Inappropriate/d Others. *In*: L. Grossberg, C. Nelson and P. Treichler, eds., *Cultural Studies*. New York: Routledge, pp. 295–337.

Hopkins, G. 1953. *Poems and Prose*. Harmondsworth: Penguin.

Hume, F. 1999. *The Mystery of a Hansom Cab*. Melbourne: Text Publishing.

Huxley, T. 1989. Struggle for Existence. *In*: P. Kropotkin, ed., *Mutual Aid: A Factor of Evolution*. Montreal: Black Rose.

Kristeva, J. 1982. *Powers of Horror: An Essay on Abjection*, L. Roudiez, trans. New York: Columbia University Press.

Lertzman, R. 2013. The Myth of Apathy: Psychoanalytic Explorations of Environmental Subjectivity. *In:* S. Weintrobe, ed., *Engaging with Climate Change: Psychoanalytic and Interdisciplinary Perspectives*, London: Routledge, pp. 117–133.

Lertzman, R. 2015. *Environmental Melancholia: Psychoanalytic Dimensions of Engagement*. London: Routledge.

Milne, A. 1958. *The World of Pooh Containing Winnie-the-Pooh and the House at Pooh Corner*. London: Methuen.

Otto, K. 2005. *Yarra: A Diverting History*. Melbourne: Text Publishing.

Pepys, S. 1972. *The Diary, Volume IV, 1663*, R. Latham and W. Matthews, ed. London: G. Bell.

Shelley, P. 1975. *The Complete Poetical Works, Volume II, 1814–1817*, N. Rogers, ed. Oxford: Clarendon Press.

Sussex, L. 2015. *Blockbuster! Fergus Hume and the Mystery of a Hansom Cab*. Melbourne: Text Publishing.

3 Alligators, crocodiles and the uncanny

Encounters between humans and crocodiles unfortunately occur in Australia with monotonous regularity and often with disastrous consequences for both parties, but also with cultural implications for how humans and animals co-habit planet earth. This is especially the case for the way in which crocodiles are portrayed, including in the Bible and usually as some sort of monster. For instance, in north Queensland in October 2004 a crocodile attacked a man in a tent and dragged him out of it only to be saved from a worse fate by the valiant efforts of a grandmother who jumped on the back of the croc who released the man and then proceeded to attack her. The print media headlined the story and captioned the accompanying photo with 'Gran who beat off croc attack' (2004). This headline gave a curiously Australian, and horrifyingly real, inflection to the immortal lines of a Tony Joe White song, 'Polk Salad Annie,/ gator's got your Grannie,/ chomp, chomp' (White, 1997). The newspaper story described the crocodile as 'a bloodthirsty predator.' This description of the crocodile was only jumping on the same bandwagon as its cousins in television news as they had already referred to the crocodile earlier in the week as 'the four-metre monster.' In both constructions of the crocodile as bloodthirsty predator and monster not only was its size, but also its use of its jaws and teeth as a potentially lethal weapon and the fearful possibility of being eaten was placed on the menu for the delectation of the media consumer over breakfast or dinner who could savour with relief that they were safe from being eaten.

This event and its media aftermath harks back to other incidents and representations involving crocodiles, such as Baby Bob and Steve Irwin, especially as there was a baby involved in the most recent incident. Fears for the safety of Baby Bob and the vilification of Steve Irwin from Indianapolis to Indooroopilly highlight human's fascination with, and fear of, crocodiles and their cousins, alligators. They also highlight the visceral nature of human bodily being and experience, particularly when it comes to food and feeding. With Steve holding a chicken in one hand to feed the croc and Bob in the other *not* to feed it, but with the possibility that it could feed on him, the boundary between being food and not food was evident for all to see, especially as baby and chicken were about the same size and colour. This raised fears of an oral kind about who gets to eat and who gets to be eaten.

It also raised again the horrifying possibility that a croc might take a baby, just as a dingo took one, too, as with Azaria Chamberlain in 1980. And just as she was taken from a tent, so in the most recent case the baby was in the tent. As in the Lindy Chamberlain case, the Steve Irwin case also brought about the equally terrifying actuality of another moral panic and trial by media with Steve accused of careless parenting like Michael Jackson, or attempted son-icide with the croc as weapon, or accomplice, or both. The portrayal of the croc as some sort of orally sadistic monster made it well suited, if not typecast, to play this role which it has been playing for a long time – but only since humans have appeared on the earth long after it.

In this chapter I argue that the typecasting of the alligator and the croco-dile as orally sadistic monsters is a projection of human desires and fears on to these non-human beings. These desires and fears of an oral nature are tied up with the uncanny. For Freud, the alligator and the crocodile portrayed as orally sadistic monsters are vehicles and vectors of the uncanny. This combination gives rise to what could be called 'the monstrous uncanny' in which the fascinating and horrific are projected onto, and embodied in, an orally sadistic monster. The uncanny, as we saw in chapter 1, counters the aesthetics of the sublime, the picturesque (pleasing prospects) and the beautiful. Whereas the latter three privilege the distancing sense of sight, the uncanny engages the sense of smell which is much more up close and personal, though not as immediate as touch and taste. Smell is often com-mented upon in encounters, real or imagined, with an alligator or crocodile.

The monstrous uncanny, however, not only engages the olfactory but also the oral and tactile. The uncanny associated with smell (an association Freud made) is a sublimation to some extent of the uncanny associated with taste and touch. The uncanny is evoked by what is not seen, which could not only be what is smelt, but also what is tasted and touched, both of which are involved when being eaten. The fear of being killed and eaten, and the desire not to be, are understandable, and certainly characterize the human side of the relationship with alligators and crocodiles. It also presumably characterizes the other side too. The relationship between eater and eaten is ultimately non-reciprocal: only one being gets to eat and the other to be eaten. When humans venture into the habitat of alligator or crocodile they can be prey and 'being prey' as Val Plumwood describes it is a terrifying experience, but also instructive as it was for her. Being prey highlights the non-reciprocal nature of the relationship. Besides consuming alligators and crocodiles as meat, humans also consume their habitat by destroying wetlands in a colonizing and non-reciprocal relationship.

The monstrous uncanny is also associated with the colonial unconscious, whether it be with William Bartram's and John Muir's encounters with an alligator in a Florida swamp (see Giblett, 2018, chapter 4), or Plumwood's and Freud's accounts of stories about crocodiles in a New Guinea swamp (as we will see in this chapter). The return to the repressed involves a return not only to the individual's own repressed, but also to the culture's repressed. Both returns are figured in all these stories in association with the alligator or crocodile as an orally sadistic monster and the swamp as a grotesque place. Rather than reproducing this figuration of monstrosity, this chapter concludes by arguing for a relationship with alligators and crocodiles characterized by mutuality in which they and their habitat are respected and conserved. Animals, as Whatmore (2002, p. 32) advises, are 'best considered as strange persons, rather than familiar or exotic things.' In other words, they are best considered as what Haraway (2008) calls companion species, or as uncanny beings, rather than as monsters.

Alligators and crocodiles have been living on the earth for 200 million years (barely half as long as sharks) but much longer than any other currently surviving, similar-sized genus of the animal kingdom. They are truly a 'blast from the past.' As such, they are vehicles and vectors for the uncanny. Freud (1985, p. 340) defined the uncanny as 'that class of the frightening which leads back to what is known of old and long familiar.' The uncanny is not only a return to the past, but also in quasi-Freudian terms 'a return *to* the repressed,' including the colonial repressed. What was repressed for the nineteenth-century, petit-bourgeois and Viennese Freud was invariably sexual in nature.

More generally in patriarchal culture the repressed is what is corporeal, visceral, maternal and monstrous. These can include the sexual, oral and anal, all of which can be, and were, associated with the colonial. In Freud's 'The Uncanny' the crocodile emerges as a figure for the British colonial repressed to which he returns via the vehicle and vector of the artefacts of colonialism which bear the traces of other, alien or exotic places and peoples. The repressed does not have a fixed content or function but changes historically and varies culturally, though the crocodile and swamp as sites of the colonial unconscious have been with us for some time as we will see. Crocodiles for the ancient Egyptians were sacred, as they are for Australian Aboriginal peoples.

Inexplicable

Perhaps no animal has been more deified/demonized than the alligator and crocodile, the 'monarch of the marsh' and the 'king of beasts' of the tropical swamp. The alligatorian and the crocodilian have been repressed for a long time, at least since Freud's time, and it still persists. For Vollmar (1972, p. ix) 'crocodiles, alligators and caimans both horrify and fascinate.' In Freud's (1985, p. 339) terms, they are uncanny as he defined the uncanny as 'what is frightening – what arouses dread and horror' and I have defined the uncanny in chapter 1 of *Psychoanalytic Ecology* as that which is both horrifying and fascinating. Vollmar (1972, p. ix) suggests that 'lurid travellers' tales of evil reptiles lying loglike in tropical mud, ready to snatch and devour the unwary human, linger in the memory.' Freud (1985, p. 367, 2003, p. 151) developed the uncanny from reading one such tale, L. G. Moberly's 'Inexplicable,' published in *The Strand Magazine* in 1917. This story harks back to the ur-travellers' tale of alligators: Bartram's account of his travels, and encounter with alligators, in a Florida swamp first published in 1791 (see Giblett, 2018, pp. 68–69).

In his reading of Moberly's story Freud downplays the role of real alligators and ignores the swamp as the place *par excellence* of the uncanny. If I were Freud, I would psychoanalyse some long-lost and repressed memories to do with his father, identify the crocodile as some sort of phallic symbol in Freud's lexicon of symbols and conclude that Freud's reading has something to do with his mother as the swamp is a maternal place. Yet rather than psychoanalysing Freud's psychopathology, I want to analyse the psychogeopathology that portrays the alligator and the crocodile as an orally sadistic monster, to engage in the talking cure of a psychoanalytic ecology that would regard them and the swamp in less demonic and more sacral terms, and to promote ecomental health that would mean that these psychogeopathological symptoms did not arise in the first place (as I am arguing in *Psychoanalytic Ecology*).

Freud, perhaps in typical fashion, gives a three or four sentence summary of the story he 'came across' in a magazine. He does not give a reference other than saying that it appeared in 'a number of the English *Strand Magazine*' (Freud, 2003, p. 151). Some time ago I 'came across' two precise references to the story in Nicholas Royle's *The Uncanny*, one to the original publication in *The Strand Magazine* and the other to a reprint in an anthology of stories from *The Strand Magazine* (Royle, 2003, pp. 140–141, n. 3; Moberly, 1917, 1991). Rather than concentrating on the slips and mistakes in Freud's retelling as he himself would do, I want to consider the gaps and absences, the symptomatic lacunae, of Freud's reading in order to reinstate alligators and crocodiles living in a swamp as a vehicle and vector of the uncanny and disinvest their construction as orally sadistic monsters.

In 'The Uncanny' Freud (2003, p. 151) relates how:

> During the isolation of the Great War, I came across a number of the English *Strand Magazine*. In it, among a number of pointless contributions, I read a story about a young couple who move into a furnished flat in which there is a curiously shaped table with crocodiles carved in the wood. Towards evening the flat is regularly pervaded by an unbearable and highly characteristic smell, and in the dark the tenants stumble over things and fancy they see something undefinable gliding over the stairs. In short, one is led to surmise that, owing to the presence of this table, the house is haunted by ghostly crocodiles, or that the wooden monsters come to life in the dark, or something of the sort. It was quite a naïve story, but its effect was extraordinarily uncanny.

Freud makes at least two mistakes in summarizing the story, the first of which is that the young couple move into a house, not a flat, furnished only with the table ('the table goes with the house' says the agent) and the table has carvings of alligators, not crocodiles, though Moberly's story itself slips between them as crocodiles, not alligators, inhabit New Guinea which is referenced in the story. These slips may be symptomatic of something more profound and if I were Freud I would no doubt think so and would analyse them (and him) for it. I am more interested, though, in the presences and absences in Freud's account, what he reproduces correctly and what he misses out altogether. Freud is not alone in referring to alligators or crocodiles as monsters as we have heard in a recent television report and as we shall see. There is a textual warrant for doing so in that the first-person narrator of the story refers to alligators as 'loathly monsters.' Yet this is not in relation to the carved, wooden alligators on the table, but in relation to a story within the story, a traveller's tale, about real, living alligators in a swamp in New Guinea that Freud does not consider at all as if he only read half the story by Moberly (more of that shortly).

First, the table. The first-person narrator (May, the wife of Freud's 'young couple') describes the effect the carved alligators had on her:

> as the light fell on the scaly bodies they had an extraordinary look of life, and the little sinister heads with the small evil eyes almost seemed to move. I shuddered and drew away from the table.
> (Moberly, 1917, p. 573, 1991, p. 184)

May feels quite faint for a moment and says to the agent ' "there is such a queer smell in here," . . . becoming all at once conscious of a strange and penetrating odour I had not before noticed.' She begins to suggest that it might be the drains but the agent is quick to interrupt and advise that they were 'set in order before the last tenant vacated the house . . . I have the sanitary people's certificate about them' (Moberly, 1917, p. 573, 1991, p. 185). This terrace house is, however, not a working-class 'swamp' whose bad air was the supposed vector of malaria in the miasmatic theory of disease and the target of the Sanitary Movement (see Giblett, 1996 and its references). The carved figures on the table are creatures of the swamp and smell is a vector of the uncanny in the psychoanalytic theory of the psychopathology of everyday life in modernity.

May's husband Hugh's first encounter with the table is just as uncanny as hers. He runs his fingers over the carved surface of the table and rests them on the head of one of the alligators, 'a head fashioned with such skill that its loathsome naturalness made one shudder. "Good heavens, May, the things look so lifelike I could almost have sworn one of them squirmed"' (Moberly, 1917, p. 574, 1991, p. 186). Inanimate things coming to life, or seeming to do so, or imitating life, is for Freud one of the features and vectors of the uncanny.

The figuration of the alligator as 'a thing,' 'this thing' and 'the thing' persists into recent fiction as this is precisely how T. Coraghessan Boyle figures one in his 1990 novel *East is east* (Boyle, 1990, pp. 335–336). 'The Thing' has been defined by Kristeva (1989, p. 13) as:

> the real that does not lend itself to signification, the centre of attraction and repulsion, the seat of sexuality from which the object of desire will become separated . . . the Thing is an imagined sun, bright and black at the same time.

'The Thing' occupies a zone prior to and outside signification, what Kristeva (1984) elsewhere calls 'signifiance,' which is also prior to and outside the separation of subject and subject in what Kristeva (1982) also calls abject. It is a creature of the uncanny, the centre and site of fascination and horror, the vehicle and vector of the monstrous.

Hugh and May are visited by a friend called Jack Wilding for whom the carved alligators trigger memories not related by Freud in his recounting of the story, which highlights the importance of the fact that the table is located in a house, not a flat. After dinner 'on a delicious May night' the two men friends are chatting with the windows open. The spring smells of the garden waft into the room:

> when all at once the drifting sweetness from without was tainted by that same strange odour which we had noticed once or twice before. . . . As it

drifted across the room our guest suddenly sat bolt upright in his chair, and a curious greyness overspread his naturally bronzed complexion. 'My God!' he said, 'what is that? And why does it smell the same – the same – ' His sentence trailed off into silence, and in the intense stillness following his strange words I heard a sound which, for some reason I could not pretend to explain, gave me a feeling of cold fear. I can only describe the sound as like a far-away bellowing – not precisely the bellowing of cattle, but a more sinister, more horrible sound, pregnant with evil. 'You hear it too?' Jack Wilding questioned, under his breath. . . . 'And the stench is here too! Good God! If I thought I should ever have to cross that swamp again I would go mad.'

(Moberly, 1917, p. 576, 1991, p. 190)

The immediacy of the sense of smell takes Jack back to what was old and long familiar, and to what was long forgotten, if not repressed. Jack then recovers himself sufficiently to say:

'I must have had a nightmare – a waking nightmare,' he said, looking around him. 'I could have sworn that I smelt the alligator swamp in New Guinea, the place where –' He broke off short. 'I heard the loathsome brutes bellowing,' he began again; 'but, of course – or course, it was merely some association of ideas.'

(Moberly, 1917, p. 577, 1991, p. 190)

Hugh indicates the table and suggests that it was the trigger for Jack's association of ideas:

Jack turned and glanced at the table, and he recoiled when he saw the grinning heads lying amongst the crusted delicacy of leaves and flowers. 'Loathsome beasts!' he said, and again his voice shook . . . I crossed an alligator swamp once with a friend. . . . It was dark, the place swarmed with those unspeakable devils, their stench was everywhere. It was dark – and poor old Danson' – he paused, as if speech were almost impossible – 'they dragged him off the path of the logs in the darkness'. . . . Somehow his words brought before me the hideous swamp, the darkness, the loathly monsters waiting for their prey, and the remembrance of just such an incident in a book I had once read flashed into my mind.

(Moberly, 1917, p. 578, 1991, p. 191)

The original *Strand Magazine* publication of the story has accompanying illustrations by Dudley Tennant, one of which is of this story within the story, complete with a glimpse of both the table and the log path, and a depiction of Jack as both the teller of the tale and character in it (Moberly, 1917, p. 577).

Jack goes on to relate how 'the place swarmed with those unspeakable devils.' Swarming creatures, in biblical terms, are 'an abomination.' They are neither fish nor flesh nor fowl. They neither just swim nor walk nor fly, but do all three. These alligators are no exception. When the wooden alligators come so life they always seem to be sliding or slithering between Jack's or Hugh's feet (but not May's, as presumably she keeps her legs together like a lady). The housekeeper later describes how they go 'slithering' and 'running on their underneaths' (Moberly, 1917, p. 574, 1991, p. 193). They do not walk on all fours like domesticated animals. They do not separate their grotesque lower bodily stratum from the grotesque lower earthly stratum, but are part and parcel of it. The abominable is also almost beyond words. It is inexplicable as the story concludes and as its title signals.

Being prey

The Australian eco-feminist and eco-philosopher Plumwood had a close encounter with a crocodile in Kakadu National Park in Northern Australia in 1985. She lived to tell the tale, though, unlike Danson, but it took some time for her to be able to tell it. I am not going to attempt to retell the story in all its details and if I attempted to sum it up by saying it was a gripping and gut-wrenching story I would be making bad puns. Plumwood's story is worth reading for itself. By reading it critically I am not belittling or demeaning her experience, which was traumatic to state the obvious, nor her individually as she was heroic to say the least. Rather, as with Freud, I am trying to critique the patriarchal and colonial elements that emerge in it despite her best efforts to keep them at bay.

Her story has some explicit elements of the uncanny, such as her description of 'the unfamiliar sensation of being watched' and her 'whispering sense of unease' prompted, not by the sight of a crocodile, but of 'a strange rock formation' (Plumwood, 1996, pp. 33–34, 1999, p. 78, 2000a, p. 57, 2000b, p. 130) which is a portent of what is to come. Plumwood hears whispers of unease and observes the strange rock formation so she is in a heightened state of sensory alertness. When the crocodile attacks her flimsy fibre-glass canoe 'the unheard of was happening' (Plumwood, 1996, p. 34, 1999, p. 78, 2000a, p. 131, 2000b, p. 57). The uncanny is evoked by hearing (or not) and smelling, by what can be heard or not, what can be smelt, but generally not by seeing. Deathly silence evokes the uncanny. In this case, being seen also evokes it. 'Being prey' as she calls it, is the result of being seen. To be prey one is eventually seen. The crocodile stalks its prey using the senses of hearing, smell and sight. Plumwood is not the subject of the gaze, but its object. She hears whispers of unease and hears (and sees) the unheard of, a crocodile attacking a canoe.

The ten-year gap between 'being prey' and publishing her account and reflections on this event under this title attests perhaps to the difficulty for her of coming to terms with her experience and expressing it. Part of the difficulty was not only the trauma of the attack itself but also the way in which her story was subjected to what she called 'the cultural drive to represent it [the attack] in terms of the masculinist monster myth: the master narrative' (Plumwood, 1996, p. 40, 1999, p. 85, 2000a, p. 139, 2000b, p. 59). In this myth, the crocodile is constructed as a ravening, orally sadistic monster who (or which) rapes and eats his (and it is always a male in the myth) innocent female victim. Yet Plumwood reproduces the myth herself when, for example, she earlier describes in lurid terms how she had 'a blurred, incredulous vision of great toothed jaws bursting from the water' that then 'seized [her] between the legs in a red-hot pincer grip' (Plumwood, 1996, p. 35, 1999, p. 79, 2000a, p. 131, 2000b, p. 57). The crocodile is figured as a monstrous, orally sadistic and reptilian cousin of 'Jaws' the monstrous shark.

Rather than only construing her experience in good ecological terms of being prey and so being a part of the food chain, Plumwood also turns in the longer version of her story to the mythology of New Guinea (and why not that of Australian Aborigines one wonders) as a way of accounting for her experience that does not merely deny or repress its mythological elements and significance. She suggests that 'crocodiles are masters of water' and goes on to argue that:

> the crocodile is an exploiter of the great planetary dualism of land and water. As Papua New Guinea writer Vincent Eri suggests in his novel, *The Crocodile*, the creature is a sort of magician: its technique is to steal the Other, the creature of the land, away into its world of water where it has complete mastery over it. Water is the key to the crocodile's power, and even large crocodiles rarely attack in its absence. The crocodile is then a boundary inhabitant.
> (Plumwood, 1996, p. 39, 1999, p. 84, 2000a, p. 137)

In other words, the crocodile, like the alligator, is a wetland inhabitant, an inhabitant of the intermediary zone between dry land and deep water that crosses 'the boundary' between land and water and upsets the dualism between them (see Giblett, 1996). Yet, like Freud who ignores the story within the story of the alligator swamp in New Guinea (and like Royle who ignores the alligators and the swamp in the story within the story), and like both who ignore these aspects as the vector and vehicle for the uncanny,

Plumwood overlooks the fact that the wetland with its distinctive features is the crocodile's habitat. She describes the latter as 'the swamp' and contrasts that with 'Kakadu's wetlands' with their 'dreamlike beauty' enticing her into 'a joyous afternoon's idyll' at the beginning of the story. She describes how here she 'glutted' herself on 'the magical beauty [. . .] of the lily lagoons untroubled by crocodiles' (Plumwood, 1996, p. 33, 1999, p. 76, 2000a, p. 128, 2000b, p. 56). She moralizes the pastoral world of the wetland as good and heavenly – good enough to eat with herself as metaphorical glutton – and the swamp as bad and hellish, the place of the orally sadistic and gluttonous crocodile. For her, the crocodile lives in a swamp whereas the tourist visits a wetland; in brief, swamp is bad, wetland is good.

Naturally, she would rather eat than be eaten (and wouldn't we all?). Just as she is being watched, but prefers to watch, so she prefers to 'eat' the beauty gluttonously than to be eaten greedily by the crocodile. Who can blame her? The point is, though, oral sadism rules, okay? She is a metaphorical glutton and the crocodile is figured as an orally sadistic monster. Tourist and crocodile are going about their normal, everyday business subscribing in both cases to the master narrative – despite Plumwood's best efforts to avoid it and do otherwise. The tourist watches (preferably without being watched) and consumes beauty gluttonously through his or her eyes without being consumed; the crocodile watches the tourist and sometimes consumes him or her through his or her mouth. Both are just doing their own thing in this mythology of modernity with its non-reciprocal and non-symbiotic positions of mastery of watching and eating, rather than being watched and eaten.

As the Kakadu wetland for Plumwood is good and heavenly, the crocodile swamp by implication is bad and hellish, though the wetland and the swamp are one and the same place – they are just figured differently. The Kakadu wetland is Eden before the Fall, or before the appearance of the serpent, here transformed into the crocodile. It is also the place of good magic, but crocodiles are excluded from this world of good magic as they bring trouble into paradise by enticing creatures of the land with bad magic into a watery grave, into a wet underworld, into its world – the swamp. The good magic is a sanitized white magic enticing Plumwood into the beautiful pastoral idyll of the wetland split off from, and valorized over, the black magic of the crocodile enticing her into the horrifying black water of the swamp. Magic is just magic, though, without the moralization. Plumwood (curiously for an ecofeminist) reproduces not only the patriarchal, Western moralization of the wetlandscape, but also its dualisms and spatial metaphysics and poetics of land and water, good and bad, white and black, heaven and hell, above and below (see Giblett, 1996).

Yet humans are not simply or exclusively creatures of the land, just as crocodiles are not simply or exclusively creatures of the water. Alligators and crocodiles are creatures who live in the two elements of earth and water, just as their wetland home mixes these elements (Strawn, 1997, p. 14; Giblett, 1996). Humans are also creatures of water as we are predominantly made up of water. Our beginnings as individuals are in the watery world of the womb and our beginnings as a species in evolutionary terms are in the womby world of water (as we saw in chapter 1; see also Giblett, 1996). Humans also have vestigial reptilian parts of the brain. Humans are meat for crocodiles (and vice versa), but we are also very distant cousins. We are both wetland creatures living on a complementary, non-dualistic planet of land and water, in short, of waterland.

Alligators and crocodiles in Haraway's (2008) terms are 'companion species' (though not in the same way as pets are) who occupy what she also calls a 'contact zone' between human beings and non-human beings (though again not in the same way as the human home, or domestic space, is for pets). The quaking zone is a contact zone between humans and non-humans (such as alligators and crocodiles in native quaking zones, and lice and rats in feral quaking zones of the trenches and of the ruined cities of world warfare and of urban slums). This contact zone can be phatic involving communication via the acts and senses of touching, smelling, hearing and seeing, or it can be phagic involving consumption via the acts of biting, chewing, etc. and the sense of taste. The phatic contact zone as a rule occurs with pets; the phagic with non-pets. If the pet becomes phagic, it ceases to be pet (and phatic) and may be 'put down.'

The uncanniness of alligators and crocodiles lies in the fact that they and modern urban humans live in the same earth-home (ecosphere), but not in the same house. Modern urban humans may live in the earthly wetland home of alligators and crocodiles, but the latter do not live in human houses and gardens as a rule. Alligators and crocodiles are (un)homely creatures, like human beings, of the terraqueous globe as Serres (1997, p. xiii) calls the earth. For Haraway (2008, p. 45) 'the familiar is always where the uncanny lurks. Further, the uncanny is where value becomes flesh again.' The familial – the family of 'Man,' the family of repitilians (including humans) – is where the alligatorian and crocodilian lurk just beneath the surface of the wetlands of the earth. Flesh is what carnivores – human, alligatorian and crocodilian – eat. The body becomes flesh in the uncanny; the value of the body is chomped into the flesh of a 'mouthful of terror-stricken humanity' as for Muir and Plumwood in the jaws of an alligator or crocodile, or of a mouthful of crocodile burger in my jaws as when I visited a crocodile farm outside Lusaka in Zambia in 2007. Eat or be eaten indeed.

Plumwood draws on Vincent Eri's novel to support her argument about crocodiles and water, but her reading has no real basis or textual warrant. Beside the perhaps customary references in the novel to 'the monstrous crocodile' and to 'the horrifying creature' (Eri, 1973, pp. 108, 113), the crocodile of the title does not figure (in two senses of the word) much in the novel. It is certainly not used, as Plumwood later suggests (1996, p. 39, 1999, p. 85, 2000a, p. 138), as:

> a metaphor for the relationship between colonised indigenous culture and colonising Western culture. If the crocodile-magician-coloniser can drag you completely into its medium, you have little chance; if you can somehow manage to retain a hold on your medium, you may survive.

If the crocodile is used in Eri's novel as a metaphor for anything, it is as a device for explaining the inexplicable, unlike for Moberly for whom the crocodile *is* the inexplicable. When Mitoro, the wife of the central character Hoiri, disappears the whole village maintains that a crocodile took her. Interestingly in one Aboriginal story the crocodile is a wife-stealer too (see Mudrooroo, 1994, p. 33). The men of the village hunt down a crocodile and Hoiri kills it in an act of revenge that he is privileged to perform as the victim. Yet at the end of the novel Hoiri encounters Mitori. She does not acknowledge him and no explanation for her leaving him is given other than that she is under the power of the magicians who also control or transform themselves into crocodiles.

The crocodile is a scapegoat onto which her sin of leaving her husband is heaped (as she cannot be found and punished) and the village is expiated. The crocodile is a creature of the wetland figured as what Lyotard called a 'scapeland,' not only in the sense of the anti- or counter-landscape but also in the sense of the sacrificial victim onto, or into, which the sins of the community are heaped and expiated (see Giblett, 1996, pp. 12–13). Perhaps in modern Western medical terms Mitoro was suffering from post-natal depression following the birth of their son and left Hoiri as a result. This would highlight the connection between melancholia and wetlands, and the creatures of the wetland. Alternatively, perhaps she simply ran away with another man. The crocodile-magician is a part of indigenous culture that is not necessarily good, or acts for good, but functions to explain the inexplicable unlike in Moberly's story of this title.

The colonizer, on the other hand, is largely represented by piggish patrol officers or draconian district officers. One of them is 'referred to as "the crocodile," a title that was one of praise rather than abuse' (Eri, 1973, p. 141), presumably because of his power, cruelty and ugliness. He is monstrous and horrifying like the crocodile. The colonizer certainly wants to drag the indigine into his medium represented by patrols, prisons, cities and warships. The crocodile does not represent this world. It represents an unsettling liminal zone of indigenous culture that is not necessarily good or bad, but it is certainly not the colonizer's culture, or a metaphor for it other than for the monstrous, horrifying and inexplicable in it, and all cultures, as in Moberly's story.

Plumwood associates the crocodile with the relationship between colonizer and colonized; Freud associates the uncanny with an artefact of colonialism with carved crocodiles that seem to, or do, come alive. Both are associated with a New Guinea swamp. The crocodile surfaces uncannily here in an Australian eco-feminist text quoting a novel, a colonial genre, written in a colonized culture. It also emerges in Freud's Viennese cultural and psychoanalytic repressed via a British magazine as a vector for the uncanny. In both texts the crocodile surfaces as a figure for the British colonial unconscious – repressed, but returning in their slips, gaps and lacunae via the vehicle and vector of the artefacts of colonialism which bear the traces of other, alien or exotic places and peoples.

References

Boyle, T. 1990. *East Is East*. New York: Penguin.

Eri, V. 1973. *The Crocodile*. Ringwood, VIC: Penguin.

Freud, S. 1985. The 'Uncanny.' *In*: *Art and Literature*, Penguin Freud Library 14. Harmondsworth: Penguin, pp. 335–376.

Freud, S. 2003. *The Uncanny*, D. Mclintock, trans. London: Penguin.

Giblett, R. 1996. *Postmodern Wetlands: Culture, History, Ecology*. Edinburgh: Edinburgh University Press.

Giblett, R. 2018. *Environmental Humanities and Theologies: Ecoculture, Literature and the Bible*. London: Routledge.

'Gran Who Beat Off Croc Attack. 2004. *The West Australian*, 16 October, p. 40.

Haraway, D. 2008. *When Species Meet*. Minneapolis: University of Minnesota Press.

Kristeva, J. 1982. *Powers of Horror: An Essay on Abjection*, L. Roudiez, trans. New York: Columbia University Press.

Kristeva, J. 1984. *Revolution in Poetic Language*, M. Waller, trans. New York: Columbia University Press.

Kristeva, J. 1989. *Black Sun: Depression and Melancholia*, L. Roudiez, trans. New York: Columbia University Press.

Moberly, L. G. 1917. Inexplicable. *The Strand Magazine*, 54(324), pp. 572–581.

Moberly, L. G. 1991. Inexplicable. *In*: J. Adrian, ed., *Strange Tales from the Strand*. Oxford: Oxford University Press, pp. 183–195.

Mudrooroo. 1994. Crocodiles. *In*: *Aboriginal Mythology: An A-Z Spanning the History of Aboriginal Mythology from the Earliest Legends to the Present Day*. London: HarperCollins, pp. 33–35.

Plumwood, V. 1996. Being Prey. *Terra Nova*, 1(3), pp. 32–44.

Plumwood, V. 1999. Being Prey. *In*: D. Rothenberg and M. Ulvaus, eds, *The New Earth Reader: The Best of Terra Nova*. Cambridge, MA: The MIT Press, pp. 76–91.

Plumwood, V. 2000a. Being Prey. *In* J. O'Reilly, S. O'Reilly and R. Sterling, eds., *The Ultimate Journey: Inspiring Stories of Living and Dying*. San Francisco: Travelers' Tales, pp. 128–146.

Plumwood, V. 2000b. Being Prey. *UTNE Reader*, July–August, pp. 56–61.

Royle, N. 2003. *The Uncanny*. New York: Routledge.

Serres, M. 1997. *The Troubadour of Knowledge*, S. Glaser and W. Paulson, trans. Ann Arbor: University of Michigan Press.

Strawn, M. 1997. *Alligators, Prehistoric Presence in the American Landscape*. Baltimore: The Johns Hopkins University Press.

Vollmar, F. 1972. Preface. *In*: C. Guggisberg, eds., *Crocodiles: Their Natural History, Folklore and Conservation*. Mount Eliza, VIC: Wren, pp. ix–x.

Whatmore, S. 2002. *Hybrid Geographies: Natures Cultures Spaces*. London: Sage.

White, T. 1997. Polk Salad Annie. *Tony Joe White Collection* [CD]. Festival Records.

4 The uncanny urban underside

The uncanny is applicable not only to the b(l)ack waters of the swamp, but also to the dark underworld of the city which for Freud was an object, or more precisely abject, of horror and fascination. The uncanny for Freud is a feeling or state of fascination and horror evoked by the 'dark continent,' whether it be of Africa, female sexuality, the slums, the swamp, or its monstrous creatures, such as alligators or crocodiles (as we have seen in the previous chapter). The city itself manifests symptoms of its own repressed, principally the wetlands on which it was built. The city itself manifests symptoms of its own repressed, principally the wetlands on which it was built, and of its psychogeopathology to fill or drain wetlands. Symptoms of psychopathology for Freud were inscribed on the surface of the patient's body in the form of his or her behaviour. Symptoms of psychogeopathology are inscribed on the surface of the body of the earth in the form of the city and its behaviour.

City symptoms

Using Freud's theory of the symptom as inscribed on the surface of the patient's body and applying it to the city as a cultural symptom of what Leopold (1991, pp. 212–217) calls 'a land pathology,' or more precisely a psychopathology, inscribed on the surface of the earth (hence a psychogeopathology), I read the modern city, and the project of modernity, as symptomatic of what could be called a wetland pathology, or more precisely, a psychogeopathology of the will to fill wetlands. By 'speaking the symptom' Freud believed the symptom would disappear. But speaking the symptom will not, as Sofoulis (1992, pp. 376–394) argues, simply make the symptom disappear.

For Freud (1973, p. 323), 'the task of a psychoanalytic treatment . . . is to make conscious everything that is pathogenically unconscious . . . and to fill up all the gaps in the patient's memory, to remove his amnesias.' In other words, to fill up, and so fill in, the lacunae (lagoon) in the surfaces of the patient's memory about the womb/wetlands as the place from whence we came and as the underside of the city and thus to repeat colonizing writing. The task of psychoanalytic ecology, on the other hand, would be to read the absences in the maps of the wetlands/womb as symptomatic of a psycho-geopathology of the will to fill wetlands, and so decolonize writing.

Even though the city will not disappear just because it is spoken that it is symptomatic of a repression of the swamp, speaking the city as the symptom of psychogeopathology is a kind of cultural 'talking cure' which raises the swamp as (a figure of) the cultural unconscious, indeed the cultural repressed, to consciousness and de-pathologizes it. Without that 'conscious-ness raising,' without that 'speaking the symptom,' wetlands conservation and rehabilitation will not be addressing the cultural conditions of possibil-ity of wetlands colonization and destruction, and will merely be attempting to block a tide of culturally habituated opinion going against it.

If the city is a symptom, it has a repressed. Beneath the surface of the city is the repressed of the city. Lefebvre (1991, p. 36) has wondered:

> if it turned out . . . that every society, and particularly . . . the city, had an underground and repressed life, and hence an 'unconscious' of its own, there can be no doubt that interest in psychoanalysis, at present on the decline, would get a new lease on life.

Along similar lines Paul Carter (1987, p. 84) has argued that 'psychoanaly-sis borrows its imagery from the realm of space. And who is to say that the spatiality of discourse of the unconscious is merely a figure of speech?' Equally, who is to say that the unconscious as swamp is merely a figure of speech? Psychoanalytic ecology gives psychoanalysis, or at least some selected aspects of it along these lines, a new lease on life.

The city has a repressed in the form of the sewerage system beneath it. Some cities have repressed the swamps on which they are built. The rela-tionship between cities and wetlands has been a close but vexed one, espe-cially in modern times: some cities, such as Paris and St Petersburg, were built on land reclaimed from marshes, whereas other cities, such as Venice 'canalised' their wetlands (see Giblett, 2016a) and some new colonial set-tlements which grew into cities, such as Perth (Western Australia) (Giblett, 2013, chapter 15) and Melbourne (Victoria) (Giblett, 2016b), were founded between a river and swamps. These cities could only expand in an unin-terrupted fashion by filling or draining the swamps. The slums of other, especially industrial, cities were built on marshes: Mosside in Manchester, the Bogside in Londonderry (even the names are indicative of their wetland sites), and much of the East End of London.

The project of colonization, especially in its modern phase and especially in relation to the establishment of settlements and the foundation of cities, is strongly tied to the drainage or filling of wetlands; in fact, the latter makes possible the former. Without the draining or filling of wetlands the establishment and expansion of many modern cities would not have been possible (see Giblett, 2016a). Modern cities sublimate the slimy or swampy (see Figure 1.1, p. 4). Their skyscrapers raise the city above the swampy; their height represses the depths; their suburbs spread out, filling the wetlands, or more recently, aestheticising them in accordance with the conventions of English park land. As far as cities go, the project of modernization has been to fill or drain wetlands. Wetlands have posed and still pose an obstacle to urban development. In order for development to take place wetlands are filled in order to create a smooth and replete surface on which development can then take place.

The swamps beneath, or before, the city are repressed spatially and historically. Reading old maps of the city in terms of the way in which they repress swamps enables that history to come to light. The map was a powerful instrument of colonization in the hands of early explorers, surveyors and settlers but is now a significant symptom of their will to fill wetlands. The historical repressed of the city, the swampy history which the city would like to forget it had, is decolonized in the psychoanalytic reading of the map. Psychoanalysis can be given a new lease of life by raising the unconscious, indeed repressed, of the city to consciousness and by a psychoanalytic ecology which would undertake a cultural talking cure of the psychogeopathology of the will to fill, or aestheticise, or create artificial, wetlands.

Although the city will not disappear as symptom of the psychogeopathology of the will to fill, the wetland as a psychogeopathological category of the horrific and the monstrous may do. The possibility of a psychoanalytic cultural studies has repeatedly been entertained in order to address the cultural unconscious so often neglected by mainstream cultural studies. Yet a psychoanalytic cultural (and environmental) studies would not simply be diagnostic of the cultural (and environmental) unconscious. It would also be a talking cure of the cultural symptom which will not make the symptom disappear but would undermine the conditions of possibility of its pathological repetition.

The colonial map is distinguished by the politics of presence and absence, by what gets plotted or named and what does not. Either way, the colonial map reduces space, and the Earth, including wetlands, to a flat surface of inscription. In and by this process the depths of the wetland are repressed. Surfaces of inscription, Lyotard (1984, p. 98; my emphasis) argues, are 'themselves flows of stabilized quiescent libidinal energy, functioning as *locks*, *canals*, regulators of desire, as its figure-producing figures.' The reduction of the depths of the Earth in general and of wetlands in particular to the surface of the map and the surface of the Earth regulates the nether(wet)lands of the unconscious. Yet this reduction of depth to surface is, Deleuze and Guattari (1977, p. 11) argue, a necessary condition for social reproduction: 'some kind of full body, that of the earth or the despot, a recording surface, an apparent objective movement, a fetishistic, perverted, bewitched world are characteristic of all types of society as a constant of social reproduction.' In the case of wetlands, the Earth is constituted as full body by *not* having its wetlands marked on maps and/or by having its wetlands filled in.

As a consequence of this process of producing a full body, the earth is, Deleuze and Guattari (1977, p. 141) go on to argue, 'the surface on which the whole process of production is inscribed.' Although the Earth may be covered with water, it is still a surface for the inscription, or writing, of colonization and development. Writing for Michel de Certeau (1984, pp. 134–135) is:

> the concrete activity that consists in constructing on its own, blank space (*un espace propre*) – the page – a text that has power over the exteriority from which it has first been excluded . . . it allows one to act on the environment and transform it . . . it is capitalist and conquering. . . . And so is the modern city: it is a circumscribed space in which . . . the will to make the countryside conform to urban models is realised.

The page of the colonial map has power over the wetlands which it has excluded. It constitutes the wetlands as object, or more precisely abject (to use Kristeva's term (1982)) to be 'managed' and transformed.

Although writing has power, this power is relative as writing is subject, in turn, to the power of speech. In a number of places Jacques Derrida (1976, p. 3) has argued along the lines that 'the history of truth,' or at least the Western history of (Western) truth (there is a high degree of lexical redundancy here), 'of the truth of truth, has always been . . . the debasement of writing, and its repression outside "full" speech.' As a result, writing has become synonymous, or at least associated, with other 'Western' repressions. Writing, in Derrida's (1976, p. 35) terms, 'the letter, the sensible inscription, has always been considered by Western tradition as the body and matter external to the spirit, to breath, to speech, and to the logos.' In terms of colonialism, writing is the messy and corporeal colonial process, the 'white's man burden,' external to and repressed by the civilization and enlightenment of the colonizing nation yet necessary for and to it. In terms of the natural environment, the wetland, the swamp, the marsh, has invariably been considered by the patriarchal Western tradition as the *lower* body and *dead* matter, the grotesque lower bodily and earthly stratum, external to writing, to the mark, the inscription, and doubly external to speech, spirit, etc., to the colonial centre and seat of power.

Yet the colonial process of writing does not master a compliant and passive object but tries to master an active agent which is a threat to the colonizing power, particularly in the form of the wetland. The repression of writing is referred to elsewhere by Derrida (1978, p.197) 'as the repression of that which threatens presence and the mastering of absence.' The colonies threaten the presence of the 'home' power and its mastering of the absence of home and the homely in the colonies, especially in the unhomely swamps. This threat is posed by the return of the repressed via the empire writing back or leaving traces on surface of the clean and proper body of the surveyor (William Byrd) or the philosopher (Jean Paul Sartre) by immersion in the slimy and swampy (for Byrd and Sartre, see Giblett (1996)). Writing as inscription on the surfaces of the body and the (wet)land is the instrument of colonization; writing as trace in the depths of the body, the slimy and the swampy is a threat to colonization. There are not two sorts of writing, but writing is double or split between the primal writing of the trace and the colonial writing of the inscription both of which always coexist and can take place on the surface of the body and the land. The writing of the map masters the absence of home and the map, in turn, is mastered by the speech of the colonial power. But the unhomely repressed threatens the homely and always returns in cultural dreaming, such as slips, tropes and bungled actions.

A distinction is to be drawn between what Derrida (1978, p. 197) describes in a chapter on 'Freud and the Scene of Writing' as 'the mastering of absence as speech and the mastering of absence as writing.' Yet the two masteries are linked and operate in conjunction with each other in that mastery of speech masters writing, and the mastering of absence as speech masters writing's mastering of absence. Explorer-mapmakers master absence, the absence of 'home,' of Europe, by writing journals and drawing maps. This writing is mastered, in turn, by the speech of colonial administrators and secretaries who doubly master the absence of home in the colonies mediated through the colonizing process of map and journal. The colonial power holds the colonized lands at arm's length by articulating and mediating its power through writing. Besides a double process of mastery, there is also a double process of repression in which speech represses writing which in turn represses the land in general and the wetland in particular. As writing is the repressed of speech, so the swampy and the slimy are the repressed of writing. They threaten to return and to mark the body of the writer. Perhaps the slime and the swamp are such powerful figures for the unconscious because they are doubly repressed (see Figure 1.1, p. 4).

If writing is colonizing, especially via map-making, then speaking the symptom and undertaking a cultural 'talking cure' will be decolonizing rather than merely deconstructive. Yet to restore the symptom to full speech as Freud does would be tantamount to recolonizing the already colonized. It would be to re-assert colonial power in the very act of deciphering its symptoms. Colonization writes on surfaces, not only on the surface of the 'native's' and the convict's body, but also on the surface of the earth via the city and the map. Franz Kafka's story 'In the Penal Colony,' or variously translated as 'In the Penal Settlement,' is a graphic and horrific depiction of the convict's body as literally a surface of inscription for colonial law. Decolonization reads these surfaces for their symptomatic manifestation of the cultural repressed and the economic and political oppressed. Speaking the symptom of the city and the map decolonizes the wetland.

The inscription of the city plan on the surface of the page and of the city itself on the surface of the earth, including the wetland, can be read in Freudian terms as a cultural symptom which manifests the repressed (see Figure 1.1, p. 4). In Lectures 17 and 18 of the *Introductory Lectures*, Freud theorizes the symptom as having a sense inscribed on the surface of the patient's body. Likewise, more recently Jacques Lacan (1977, p. 166) saw a symptom as 'a metaphor in which flesh or function is taken as a signifying element.' If symptoms are inscribed on surfaces, as Freud contends, then they are a sort of writing. Conversely, Derrida (1982, p. 110) argues that 'writing belongs to the order and exteriority of the symptom.' Extrapolating more generally from Freud, Derrida and Lacan, and taking further Deleuze and Guattari's suggestion that a surface of inscription is necessary for social reproduction and that the earth is one such surface, a symptom can be inscribed on any surface – bodies, the earth, pages, etc. – and a symptom is cultural irrespective of whether it is inscribed on an individual body, e.g. anorexia nervosa, or on the earth, e.g. cities in or on former swamps. These symptoms are constructed from unconscious processes and are symptomatic of what Sofoulis (pers. comm.) calls an arrested or blocked process which dam the flows of the libido and stem the tides of desire.

The process of arresting or blocking is pathological. A symptom for Freud (1979, p. 237) 'actually denotes the presence of some pathological process.' Manifested in the symptom of the city and the map, and repressed by them, is the psychogeopathology of the colonization of nature in general and of wetlands in particular. The marks which colonialism leaves on its maps and the marks its cities leave on the earth are symptomatic of a psychogeopathology. A pathology is indicated in general, as Leopold (1991, p. 217) points out, by 'self-accelerating rather than self-compensating departures from normal functioning.' In the case of a land pathology in particular this self-acceleration occurs in the 'collective organism of land and society.'

The growth of cities has certainly been self-accelerating over the last one hundred years. The twenty-first century is what Joel Kotkin (2005, p. xvii) calls 'an urban century, the first where a majority of people live in cities.' Indeed, Eric Sanderson (2009, p. 33) notes that '2007 marked the first time in human history that more people lived in cities than in rural areas.' Cities have departed from the normal, indigenous functioning of the land/society organism, not least in the relationship with wetlands which had obtained, in Australia for example, for 50 000 years before (McComb and Lake, 1990, pp. 13–23).

The return of the repressed can be seen in Freud's own anecdote in 'The Uncanny.' Strolling in a small Italian town and ending up in its red-light district can evoke the uncanny, such as when Freud (2003, p. 144) relates in 'The Uncanny' how he was:

> Strolling one hot summer afternoon through the empty and to me unfamiliar streets of a small Italian town. I found myself in a district about whose character I could not long remain in doubt. Only heavily made-up women were to be seen at the window of the little houses, and I hastily left the narrow street at the next turning. However, after wandering about for some time without asking the way, I suddenly found myself back in the same street, where my presence began to attract attention. Once more I hurried away, only to return there again by a different route. I was now seized by a feeling that I can only describe as uncanny, and I was glad to find my way back to the piazza that I had recently left and refrain from any further voyages of discovery.

Freud's lost object is himself that he repeatedly finds in the wrong place, or more precisely, the place to which he unintentionally returns. This return enacts an unconscious desire. The uncanny is a return *to* the repressed. In Freud's autobiographical anecdote the repressed is not only his sexual repressed, but also the morally and spatially repressed of the small Italian town, its red-light district, to both of which he keeps on returning.

In Freud's autobiographical anecdote the repressed is not only his sexual repressed, but also the morally and spatially repressed of the small Italian town, its red-light district. The sexually and spatially repressed is the bodies of the prostitutes embodying what Rebecca Solnit (2000, p. 209) calls 'transformation of city into female body.' For the young Walter Benjamin (1979, pp. 330–331, 1999b, p. 623) the city of Berlin is transformed into the body of servant girls. He relates how:

> The dream ship that came to fetch us on those evenings must have rocked at our bedside on the waves of conversation, or under the spray

of clattering plates, and in the early morning it set us down on the ebb of the carpet beating that came in at the window with the moist air on rainy days and engraved itself more indelibly in the child's memory than the voice of the beloved in that of the man – this carpet beating that was the language of the nether world of servant girls, the real grownups, a language that sometimes took its time, languid and muted under the grey sky, breaking at others into an inexplicable gallop, as if the servants were pursued by phantoms. The courtyard was one of the places where the city opened itself to the child.

The languid and muted language of the servant girls is not only their spoken language but also the body language of their carpet-beating that was vaguely arousing and sexually enticing for the young Walter with its overtones of sadism on the part of the servant girls and masochism on Benjamin's. The courtyard, rather than being an entry into private domestic space of the home, was a passage going out into the public space of the city, and into the female body culminating in his later depiction of, as Solnit (2000, p. 209) puts it, 'Paris as labyrinth . . . whose centre is a brothel.' The city for Benjamin is generally a labyrinthine female body.

Uncanny Paris

Benjamin specifically figured Paris as a labyrinthine whore. In *The Arcades Project* Benjamin (1999a, p. 523) cites a nineteenth-century account of 'the true Paris [which] is by nature a dark, miry, malodourous city . . . swarming with blind alleys . . . and . . . with labyrinths that lead you to the devil.' The city for Benjamin is ultimately a labyrinthine female body. Indeed, for Benjamin (1999a, p. 519) the darkness of the streets 'greatly resembles the lap of a whore.' The sexually and spatially repressed is the bodies of the prostitutes embodying what Solnit (2000, p. 209) calls his 'transformation of city into female body.' Benjamin (1999b, pp. 141–143) also figures 'Paris as Goddess.' In writing about Paris, especially in his labyrinthine, monumental and monstrous *Arcades Project*, a *femme fatale* of a book, Benjamin was primarily interested in Paris as 'the capital of the nineteenth century' as he put it, and in critiquing, as Charles Baudelaire put it, 'the goddess of Industry' (cited by Benjamin, 1973, p. 79) figured as an orally sadistic monster with her 'jaws' that consume rather than celebrating the 'goddess of the city,' as Benjamin also put it (1999b, p. 143), in the preceding centuries going back to its beginnings as Lutetia as an orally satisfying mother of the marsh.

Paris is a swamp city. It was a swamp city before it became a modern city and before it became the capital of the nineteenth century, modernity and the universe. Like a number of other swamp cities and marsh metropolises,

Paris has a slimy beginning that has largely been forgotten, but whose traces still remain. Unlike a number of other such cities, however, yet like London, the swampy beginnings of Paris can be found in the original name of Lutetia for the site for the city and then for the city itself. 'The muddy etymology of Lutetia' is linked for (Jones, 2005, p. 4) to 'the Celtic word for marshland and to *lutum*, Latin for mud.' More specifically for Andrew Hussey (2006, pp. 3, 7) Lutetia is Celtic for 'the place of mud, marshes and swamp.' The muddy aetiology of Lutetia itself is also linked to what Jones (2005, p. 4) calls 'marshy and muddy land' (for further discussion of Paris as Lutetia, see Giblett, 2016a, chapter 3).

Traces of the swamp can be found in the *Arcades Project*. Baudelaire's writings are one of the central proof texts for Benjamin with good reason. Baudelaire for Benjamin (1973, p. 81) performs the labours of Hercules to 'give shape to modernity.' Benjamin does not mention that one of Hercules's labours was to kill the brazen-beaked Stymphalian birds that lived in a swamp and are figured as orally sadistic monsters. Benjamin's Herculean labour was to kill the monstrous goddess of industry, rather than to celebrate the Lutetian mother goddess of the marsh. The buried wetland history of Paris as Lutetia also returns in Baudelaire's figuring of 'the mire of the macadam,' *la fange du macadam* (cited by Berman, 1988, p. 156). Berman (1988, pp. 160–161) relates how '*la fange* is not only a literal word for mud; it is also a figurative word for mire, filth, vileness, corruption, degradation, all that is foul and loathsome.' In and with the modern city all that is solid not only 'melts,' or is sublimated, into air, but also is desublimated, or 'melts,' into slime.

The buried wetland history of Paris as Lutetia also returns in Benjamin's figuring of the Paris of Baudelaire's poems as 'a sunken city, and more submarine than subterranean' (Benjamin, 1973, p. 171). Benjamin goes on to refer to 'the chthonic elements of the city,' such as 'its topographical formation, the old abandoned bed of the Seine.' Paris rests, or floats, on the old bed of the Seine. The motto for Paris is 'it floats but does not sink' as depicted in its coat of arms with its Latin motto (Horne, 2002, illustration following 138). Paris, however, is not a floating city like Tenochtitlán (see Giblett 2016a, chapter 1). Paris appears to be a floating city like Venice, but it is actually built on land, also like Venice. Hussey (2006, p. 7) relates that 'one of the most popular Christianized myths was that Lutetia was founded by Lucus, the seventeenth descendant of Noah, who came here to make a city on the water.' The city would have been a kind of ark, full of the goods and beasts of the earth, appearing to float on water like Venice. The famous Situationist graffiti slogan of May 1968, '*au dessous les paves, la plage*' (beneath the pavement lies the beach; cited by Smith, 2012, p. 274) should be revised to be '*au dessous les paves, lutetia*' (beneath the pavement, lies the filthy marsh).

Lutetia is remembered in the name of the Hotel Lutetia that opened in Paris in 1910 and is still operating. Benjamin (1999a, p. 516) acknowledges 'the unconquerable power in the names of streets, squares, and theaters, a power which persists in the face of all topographic replacement.' How much more so does the unconquerable power of the name of Lutetia not only persist in the name of a hotel, but also endures in the massive topographic replacement of the filthy marsh of Lutetia by the city of Paris?

Benjamin's account of Paris focuses on the culture and history of the city in the nineteenth century, a big enough undertaking as the sheer bulk of *The Arcades Project* demonstrates. Yet his lack of attention to the matrifocal pre-history of the site for the city, especially when it re-emerges in the literature of the nineteenth century, is somewhat surprising given his interest in the work of J. J. Bachofen (1967) on 'mother right,' or the Great Goddess, expressed both in *The Arcades Project* (Benjamin, 1999a, p. 361) and elsewhere in his review of Bachofen's book on the topic (Benjamin, 1996, pp. 426–427) and in his essay on Kafka written on the tenth anniversary of Kafka's death (Benjamin, 1999b, pp. 808–809).

If Benjamin had been aware of the beginnings of Paris in the swamps of Lutetia, or the meaning of the name, he may have made the connection between the work of Bachofen, the history of Paris as manifested in *The Arcades Project* (Benjamin, 1999a), and its pre-history. Regrettably he does not make this connection. Bachofen, as Benjamin points out, discusses the 'hetaeric stage' of the pre-patriarchal or matrifocal 'Mother Right,' or 'Great Goddess,' of 'the swamp world,' when the world was swamp (as Benjamin puts it in writing about Kafka; Benjamin, 1999b, pp. 808–809). Benjamin (1999b, p. 809) comments that 'the fact that this stage is now forgotten does not mean that it does not extend into the present. On the contrary: it is present by virtue of its very oblivion.'

Nineteenth-century French literature manifests not only this forgetting as the Great Goddess is not mentioned in it, but also this extension into the present as Lutetia is frequently invoked. Benjamin does not make the connection between the two. The past of what Benjamin calls 'the dark, deep womb' of what Bachofen calls (citing Arnobius) 'dirty voluptuousness (*luteae voluptates*)' (Benjamin, 1999b, p. 809) is present in the past name of Paris, *Lutetia*, not merely as dirty voluptuousness, but as dirty *swampy* voluptuousness, or, as Deleuze (1989, p. 52) puts it in his book on Bachofen, 'the lustful chaos of primeval swamps.' The reminder in the present of the past name of Paris as Lutetia 'takes us back,' as Benjamin puts it, to the past of the swamp world in which Paris began, the world of the Great Goddess, though Benjamin forgets about this too. The present figuring of Paris as

Goddess takes us back to when Lutetia the swamp was the Goddess, and not just merely figured as such.

The repressed, rich dark past of Paris swamps also returns in a one-act vaudeville performance in which, as Benjamin (1999a, p. 56) puts it, 'Lutèce emerges from the bowels of the earth, at first in the guise of an old woman.' The editors of *The Arcades Project* briefly note that 'Lutèce' is the 'Roman name for Paris' (Benjamin, 1999a, p. 959, n. 12), whereas it was previously the Celtic name for the wetland place. Similarly, in their 'Guide to Names and Terms' the editors of *The Arcades Project* gloss 'Lutèce' as 'ancient name for Paris. From Latin *Lutetia* ("city of mud")' (Benjamin, 1999a, p. 1038). However, as Benjamin (1999a, p. 83) says later (and as we have seen), 'Lutetia Parisorum,' not just Lutetia, is 'the old Roman city.' In the vaudeville performance that Benjamin paraphrases Lutetia is an old woman; in Bachofen's terms, she is the Great Goddess who lives in the bowels of the earth, the swamps.

One of the ways in which for Benjamin the hetaeric stage extends into the present is as a point of ecological critique of the present. For him,

> the murderous idea of the exploitation of nature, which has ruled over things since the nineteenth century . . . could have no place so long as the prevailing image of nature was that of the ministering mother, as reflected in Bachofen's conception of matriarchal societies.
>
> (Benjamin, 1999a, p. 361)

The green or eco-critical Benjamin has not been noted or commented upon much by Benjamin scholars, nor by eco-critics and environmental theorists either for that matter (for an exception, see Mules, 2014).

How ironic that the rule of 'the murderous idea of the exploitation of nature' should have its beginnings for Benjamin not only in the nineteenth century, but also in Paris as 'the capital of the nineteenth century' whose original name of Lutetia is precisely that of 'the ministering mother' of the swamp world. Lutetia in Benjamin's terms is 'a dialectical image' for, as he goes on to elaborate, 'while the relation of the present to the past is a purely temporal, continuous one, the relation to what-has-been to the now is dialectical: is not progression but image, suddenly emergent' (Benjamin, 1999a, p. 462). Lutetia is the dialectical image of the what-has-been of Paris as marsh and of the now of recognizability of Paris as metropolis, between the filthy marsh and the miry city. Marsh and metropolis come together dialectically in the image of Lutetia, of Paris as marsh metropolis. The dialectical image is akin to the uncanny as the return of and to the repressed, the Marxist historical materialist counterpart to the Freudian psychoanalytic uncanny.

Benjamin (1999a, p. 464) elaborates further that 'in the dialectical image, what has been within a particular epoch is always, simultaneously, "what has been from time immemorial".' Lutetia has been from time immemorial and has been in the particular epoch of the beginnings of the history of Paris. 'The dialectical image' for Benjamin (1999a, p. 474) is 'the primal phenomenon of history.' Lutetia is the primal phenomenon of the history of Paris. Of course, Lutetia can be and has been forgotten by the majority of the residents of Paris, but that does not mean, as Benjamin says, that 'it does not extend into the present. On the contrary, p. it is present by virtue of its very oblivion,' as Benjamin (1999b, p. 809) said of the hetaeric stage and Bachofen's conception of matrifocal societies (Bachofen, 1967). Lutetia extends into the present and is present by virtue of its very oblivion in Paris today and in it and other marsh metropolises and swamp cities. Benjamin's comment is a reminder of the motto for Paris ('it floats but does not sink'), as well as a fitting motto for the return of the repressed in nature and culture.

The modern city not only takes place in a place in space but also occurs in a moment in time, in a period of history. The hell of the modern city is not only found in the city itself, in its dark and dirty places, but also in the hell of the modern, in its hot and fetid events. Modernity for Benjamin (1999a, p. 842; see also 1999a, p. 544) is 'the time of hell.' Why? Because 'the eternity of hell' is constituted by the fact 'that which is newest . . . remains, in every respect, the same.' The modern is cut off from pre-history and is constituted by its severance from pre-history. Most residents of all the cities discussed in *Cities and Wetlands* (Giblett, 2016a) have no knowledge of the pre-history of the city in which they live. Benjamin (1999a, p. 544) earlier on the same page defined the 'modern' as 'the new in the context of what has always already been there.' The modern city in general, and Paris in particular, are new in the context of the swamp that has always already been there.

The temple of Lutetia of the grotesque lower earthly and bodily strata (as Mikhail Bakhtin (1984, chapters 5 and 6) called the latter), of the monstrous feminine *was* the swamp, whereas the arcades are temples of the God of greedy capitalism, of the capital(ist) city, of new, modern, monumental Paris. The arcades, or interior passageways, of Paris in the nineteenth century for Benjamin (1999a, pp. 37, 546), are 'the hollow mold form which the image of "modernity" was cast' and 'temples of commodity capital.' The city/monster displaces and takes over the place of the swamp/monster. Benjamin cites an illustrated guide to Paris of 1852 in which 'an arcade is a city, even a world, in miniature' (cited by Benjamin, 1973, p. 37, 158). An arcade is a miniature city and world of commodity capitalism that displaces and replaces the macro-earth and economy of swamps and marshes that nevertheless leave traces in the history of, and metaphors for the city of Paris, and its sewers, and its pre-history as marsh.

References

Bachofen, J. 1967. *Myth, Religion and Mother Right: Selected Writings*, R. Manheim, trans. Princeton: Princeton University Press.

Bakhtin, M. 1984. *Rabelais and His World*, H. Iswolsky, trans. Bloomington: Indiana University Press.

Benjamin, W. 1973. *Charles Baudelaire: A Lyric Poet in the Era of High Capitalism*, H. Zohn, trans. London: Verso.

Benjamin, W. 1979. *One-Way Street and Other Writings*, E. Jephcott and K. Shorter, trans. London: NLB.

Benjamin, W. 1996. *Selected Writings, Volume 1: 1913–1926*, M. Bullock and M. Jennings, eds. Cambridge, MA: The Belknap Press of Harvard University Press.

Benjamin, W. 1999a. *The Arcades Project*, H. Eiland, trans. Cambridge, MA: The Belknap Press of Harvard University Press.

Benjamin, W. 1999b. *Selected Writings, Volume 2: 1927–1934*, M. Jennings, H. Eiland and G. Smith, eds. Cambridge, MA: The Belknap Press of Harvard University Press.

Berman, M. 1988. *All That Is Solid Melts into Air: The Experience of Modernity*. New York: Penguin.

Carter, P. 1987. *The Road to Botany Bay: An Essay in Spatial History*. London: Faber.

Certeau, M. de 1984. *The Practice of Everyday Life*, S. Rendall, trans. Berkeley: University of California Press.

Deleuze, G. 1989. *Masochism: Coldness and Cruelty*. New York: Zone Books.

Deleuze, G. and F. Guattari, 1977. *Anti-Oedipus: Capitalism and Schizophrenia*, R. Hurley, M. Seem and H. Lane, trans. New York: Viking Press.

Derrida, J. 1976. *Of Grammatology*, G. Spivak, trans. Baltimore: The Johns Hopkins University Press.

Derrida, J. 1978. *Writing and Difference*, Allan Bass, trans. London: Routledge and Kegan Paul.

Derrida, J. 1982. *Dissemination*, B. Johnson, trans. London: Athlone.

Freud, S. 1973. *Introductory Lectures on Psychoanalysis*, Penguin Freud Library 1. Harmondsworth: Penguin.

Freud, S. 1979. *On Psychopathology: Inhibitions, Symptoms and Anxiety and Other Works*, Penguin Freud Library 10. Harmondsworth: Penguin.

Freud, S. 2003. *The Uncanny*, D. Mclintock, trans. London: Penguin.

Giblett, R. 1996. *Postmodern Wetlands: Culture, History, Ecology*. Edinburgh: Edinburgh University Press.

Giblett, R. 2013. *Black Swan Lake: Life of a Wetland*. Bristol: Intellect Books.

Giblett, R. 2016a. *Cities and Wetlands: The Return of the Repressed in Nature and Culture*. London: Bloomsbury.

Giblett, R. 2016b. The Lost and Found Wetlands of Melbourne. *Victorian Historical Journal*, 87(1), pp. 134–155.

Horne, A. 2002. *Seven Ages of Paris*. New York: Random House.

Hussey, A. 2006. *Paris: The Secret History*. New York: Bloomsbury.

Jones, C. 2005. *Paris: Biography of a City*. London: Penguin.

Kotkin, J. 2005. *The City: A Global History*. New York: Random House.

Kristeva, J. 1982. *Powers of Horror: An Essay on Abjection*, L. Roudiez, trans. New York: Columbia University Press.

Lacan, J. 1977. *Écrits: A Selection*, Alan Sheridan, trans. London: Tavistock.

Lefebvre, H. 1991. *The Production of Space*, Donald Nicholson-Smith, trans. Oxford: Blackwell.

Leopold, A. 1991. Land Pathology. *In:* S. Flader and J. Callicott, eds., *The River of the Mother of God and Other Essays*, Madison: University of Wisconsin Press, pp. 212–217.

Lyotard, J-F. 1984. *Driftworks*, Roger McKeon, ed. New York: Semiotext(e).

McComb A. and P. Lake. 1990. Aboriginal Use of Wetlands. *In: Australian Wetlands*. North Ryde: Angus and Robertson, pp. 13–23.

Mules, W. 2014. *With Nature: Nature Philosophy as Poetics through Schelling, Heidegger, Benjamin and Nancy*. Bristol: Intellect Books.

Sanderson, E. 2009. *Mannahatta: A Natural History of New York City*. New York: Harry N. Abrams.

Smith, P. 2012. *City: A Guidebook for the Urban Age*. London: Bloomsbury.

Sofoulis, Z. 1992. Hegemonic Irrationalities and Psychoanalytic Cultural Critique. *Cultural Studies*, 6(3), pp. 376–394.

Solnit, R. 2000. *Wanderlust: A History of Walking*. London: Penguin.

5   Mining and anal sadism

Coraghessan Boyle's (1987, pp. 33–34) coruscating novel, *World's End*, relates how:

> Depeyster Van Wart, twelfth heir to the Van Wart Manor, the late seventeenth-century country house that lay just outside Peterskill on Van Wart Ridge where it commanded a sweeping view of the town dump and the rushing, refuse-clogged waters of Van Wart Creek was a terraphage. That is, he ate dirt [but not just any dirt] . . . what he ate was ancestral dirt, scooped with a garden digger from the cool weatherless caverns beneath the house. Even now, as he sat idly at his ceremonial desk behind the frosted glass door at Depeyster Manufacturing, thinking of lunch, the afternoon paper and the acquisition of property, the business envelope in his breast pocket was half-filled with it. From time to time, ruminative, he would wet the tip of his forefinger and dip it furtively into the envelope before bringing it to his lips. Some smoked; others drank, cheated at cards or abused their wives. But Depeyster indulged only this one harmless eccentricity, his sole vice. He was a toddler, no more than two, when he first wandered away from his nurse . . . found the bleached paint–stripped door ajar and pushed his way into the comforting cool depths of the cellar. Silently, he pulled the door to and sat down to his first repast . . . grinding dirt between his milk teeth, shaping it with his tongue, relishing the faint faecal taste of it. . .
>
>   He was no child now. Fifty years old . . . smooth and handsome and with an accent rich with the patrician emphases of the Roosevelts, Schuylers, Depeysters and Van Rensselers who'd preceded him, scion of the Van Wart dynasty and nominal head of Depeyster Manufacturing, he was a man in the prime of life, tanned, graceful and athletic. . .

Terraphagy, or eating dirt, or more precisely eating earth, is here related to infantile development, manufacturing, masculinity and waste disposal. All these aspects can also be related to mining. Mining supplies manufacturing with the raw materials to be produced as products. Terraphagy is also a metaphor for mining as mining consumes minerals from the earth. Moreover, the metaphor is gendered as mining, manufacturing and waste disposal are masculine activities that master feminized nature. Furthermore, the psychodynamics of terraphagy are established in infancy and reinforced, repeated or overturned in adulthood. Relationships to the mother and 'Mother Earth' establish gendered identity and attitudes to mining and manufacturing. The town dump, the refuse-clogged creek and the ecosphere more generally are the sinks for the detritus, excreta and other waste products of manufacturing based on mining. Using Mary Douglas's (1966, p. 35, terms, mining, manufacturing, mastery and waste–disposal are phases in the process whereby earth becomes dirt. Wanted matter, or matter in place, becomes unwanted matter or matter out of place, in short, dirt.

Probably the most contentious or curious, or even controversial, of these conjunctions is the tie between infantile development and mining, and more generally between what Verena Conley 1997, p. 129) calls 'the relinquishing of the mother's body' and 'the technological mastery over nature' of modernity. The connection is hardly novel, though, as it was made half a century before by Klein, the so-called British psychoanalyst though born, unlike Freud, in Vienna, the capital of psychoanalysis. Her work is well known for its insights into the 'dim and shadowy recesses' (the cave or mine) of early childhood. For Klein, consuming with greed, but without gratitude, is a psychopathology in the young child's, and later the adult's, relation to the mother's body and, by extension I will argue following Sofoulis, 'Mother Earth.'

Consuming with greed and without gratitude the generosity of Mother Earth results in what Leopold called 'a land pathology.' For Leopold, one of the 'founding fathers' of the American conservation movement, pathological symptoms have developed in the collective organism of 'land and society.' Soil erosion, for example, was defined in 1939 in *The Rape of the Earth* (Jacks and Whyte, 1939, p. 26) as 'the modern symptom of maladjustment between human society and its environment.' These symptoms are pathological as they are what Leopold (1991, p. 217) calls 'self-accelerating rather than self-compensating departures from normal functioning.' Elsewhere Leopold (1972, p. 153) said that 'I believe that many of the economic forces inside the modern body-politic are pathogenic in respect to harmony with land.'

Mining certainly has been self-accelerating. In 1974 it was calculated that 'the last half-century has seen mankind [*sic*] consume more mineral resources than were used in the whole of previous history' (McDivitt and Manners, 1974, p. 4). Consumption of mineral resources has not abated in the years since this calculation was made, but has increased to the point where it rivals the previous fifty for the dubious distinction of exceeding 'the whole of previous history' and departing even further from the normal functioning of the land. Nor is this increase in consumption equitably distributed as David Suzuki (1998, p. 97) maintains that 'since 1940, Americans alone have used up as large a share of the Earth's mineral resources as all previous generations of humans put together.'

The psychodynamics and politics of mining

In this chapter I use the work of Klein, as well as that of Susan Griffin and Carolyn Merchant and a number of Aboriginal poets, such as Oodgeroo Noonuccal and others, to articulate critically the psychodynamics and politics of mining. I also use this work to analyse critically the politics and psychodynamics of the discourses employed by the mining industry and by the mineral disciplines. I argue that they construct the earth as a passive and compliant object to be exploited, and then expect the earth to absorb or hide their wastes in return. I also go on to make some modest proposals for different ways of talking about the earth. I argue for a move away from an emphasis on resource exploitation, or greed and gluttony, to a relationship of generosity and gratitude, of reciprocity and restoration. Although restoration is a buzzword in environmental and mining circles, it is not often motivated by gratitude and reciprocity, but more by a sense of duty. Instead of seeing the earth as something to exploit, the earth needs to be seen as our equivalent other, not as an inferior object, but at least as our equal in importance with which to have relations of respect and care, even learning to love it.

Masculinity, manufacturing and modern society are related to the politics of mining, especially to the gender politics of mining. Gender politics relates not only to the politics of relations between the genders but also between gendered entities. Politics is used here in the broad sense of power relations which are, as the passage from Boyle's novel shows, tied up with investments of desire (as well as capital) in, and yields of pleasure (as well as yields of ore and profits) from, 'ore bodies' (see Trigger, 1997, pp. 161–180). These power relations, investments and yields are tied up with the gender and ethnic politics of mining and its relationship with the earth as a gendered entity in both modern and traditional societies. Yet whereas traditional societies revere the earth as Great Mother and so as a living person, modern societies abuse the earth as dead matter.

Merchant and Griffin have enunciated the gender politics of mining extensively in terms of the Mother Earth figure. Merchant (1980, pp. 3–4; see also pp. 29–41) has argued that:

> for most traditional cultures, minerals and metals ripened in the uterus of the Earth Mother, mines were compared to her vagina, and metallurgy was the human hastening of the birth of the living metal in the artificial womb of the furnace – an abortion of the metal's natural growth cycle before its time.

The minerals and metals extracted from 'the womb of the Earth-Mother,' as Mircea Eliade (1971, pp. 41–42) puts it, are 'in some way *embryos* . . . [and] their extraction from the bowels of the earth is thus an operation executed before its due time.'

One traditional account of mining couched in these terms can be found in Pliny the Elder's *Natural History*. Written in the first century of the common era, Pliny (1991, pp. 30–31, p. 286) suggests that:

> Earth receives us when we are born and feeds us after birth and always supports us, and, at the very end embraces us in her bosom, sheltering us like a mother especially then, when we have been disowned by the rest of Nature. . . . What delights and affronts does she not afford mankind? She is dumped into the sea, or excavated to provide channels. She is tortured at all hours by water, iron, wood, fire, stone and crops, and by far more besides to serve our pleasure rather than our needs. Yet so that what she suffers on her surface, her outermost skin, may seem bearable by comparison, we penetrate her inmost parts, digging into her veins of gold and solver and deposits of copper and lead. We search for gems and certain very small stones by sinking shafts into the depths. We drag out Earth's entrails. . . . If there were any beings in the nether world, assuredly the tunnelling brought about by greed and luxury would have dug them up. . . . We search for riches deep within the bowels of the earth where the spirits of the dead have their abode, as though the part we walk upon is not sufficiently bountiful and productive. . . . But what she has hidden and kept underground – those things that cannot be found immediately – destroy us and drive us to the depths. As a result the mind boggles at thought of the long–term effect of draining the earth's resources and the full impact of greed. How innocent, how happy, indeed how comfortable, life might be if it coveted nothing from anywhere other than the surface of the earth – in brief, nothing except what is immediately available.

The concept/metaphor of the mineral veins of the body of Mother Earth persisted at least into the sixteenth century as Georgius Agricola (1960, pp. 12, 35, 37, 107) attests. After colonizing the surface of the earth the depths are colonized by shafting and tunnelling underground. As Walter Benjamin (1979, p. 104, 1996, p. 486) put it, 'everywhere sacrificial shafts were dug in Mother Earth.'

For traditional cultures, metals are embryos, metallurgy is an abortion and the mine, as Griffin (1978, p. 118) suggests, is a Caesarean section of Mother Earth, so even though the metals may have reached their term, they are mechanically removed from the earth. Aboriginal critics of mining in Australia have seen it in these terms. Following a tour of mining operations in the Pilbara region of Western Australia, Mudrooroo (1992, p. 1) wrote:

> Nyaninya na – na pala lidiyah.
> Unentire, the earth gapes open;
> The black womb slashed open by
> The grinning tropes of discord.
> He laughs and turns to mining out
> The fruits of her laborious love.

This produces what the next stanza calls 'the excavated abomination.'

The Nyoongar people of South-western Australia have rejected Mudrooroo's identity as an Aboriginal person. By quoting from his work I do not accept (or deny) his aboriginality. It is not up to me to decide. I do not cite his work in this and subsequent chapters as that of an Aboriginal writer or person, or not. I quote his work as it is invaluable and as his contribution to cross-cultural dialogue and understanding is enormous. In another poem in the same series entitled 'Baby – Man – Talk' Mudrooroo (1992, p. 2) extends the 'trope of discord' to describe mining as a violent abortive intervention:

> The miner cuts through the flesh, drags out the
> Writhing capillaries and empowders the blood,
> Evading any moral issues while a flame flickers
> In the contraction–expansion of the heart pillars,
> Gently throbbing out accords, discords, concords.

As Robert Thayer (1994, p. 123) puts it succinctly and graphically, 'by actually ripping open and consuming parts of the earth, consumptive technology symbolizes a wounding and consumption of the earth's "flesh".'

Klein on mining

The work of Klein can make a valuable contribution to this discussion of mining in three main ways: first, by moving away from simple metaphorics to a recognition that for the young infant the body of the mother and Mother Earth are one, and that for indigenes they are (in symbiosis with) the earth. As one Aboriginal poet, W. Les Russell (Gilbert, 1988, p. 3), puts it in a poem entitled 'The "Developers",' 'I am this Land and it is mine.' Second, by exploring the psychodynamics of the relation between the young child and the mother, and between indigenous and non-Aboriginal people and the earth. And third, by showing the implications both these have for the way in which the earth is treated in later life, primarily in terms of whether one greedily seeks gratification from it/her or gives gratitude back to it/her for its/her generosity.

Sofoulis (Sofia) has already suggested the pertinence of Klein's work on infantile development to an eco-feminist critique of patriarchal capitalist mining. She has argued that:

> Melanie Klein interpreted exploration, mining, scientific and intellec-
> tual research, and artistic production as sublimations of the infantile
> curiosity about origins ('epistemophilia') which arises before the firm
> imposition of gender roles, and is associated with infantile sadistic ten-
> dencies of oral and excremental character.
>
> (Sofia, 1989, p. 7; see also Sofoulis, 1983, 1984)

These tendencies are neither necessarily nor essentially ascribed to one gen-der rather than the other at an early age, though they are ones that typically characterize masculinity later on. Mining and infantile development can be articulated, as Sofia does, around a conceptualisation of what B. A Santama-ria (nd, ?1945), B. A., called, *The Earth – Our Mother*, an early book on land degradation in Australia closely aligned, in its title at least, with the conceptualization of Aboriginal relations to the earth. Errol West (Gilbert, 1988, p. 173), for instance, describes how 'The Breast of Mother Earth bore me' and how 'All I want is a private dying in the arms of my Mother Earth.'

As there is no firm sense of gender for the young infant, so is there no definite idea of self in relation to other things. Central to Klein's work on early childhood development is the contention that for the young infant there is no differentiation between it and the objects external to it. This contention derives from Freud (1975, p. 299) who, in his London notes of 1938, mimics the child: 'the breast is a part of me, I am the breast.' All objects are initially conflated with one another and equated with the mother, or parts of her, especially her breasts, as she/they are the primary object for the young infant.

Klein extended and developed Freud's contention by suggesting that this object does not necessarily remain unitary; indeed, it can, and does, become split. When the young infant feels frustration at not being fed on demand, or not being fed sufficiently, Klein (1986, pp. 176–177) argues that 'the mother's breast . . . to the child becomes split into a good (gratifying) and bad (frustrating) breast.' The good breast is an object of desire, or in Klein's (1986, p. 213) terms envy, for the young infant that s/he regards as completely adequate in fulfilling that desire:

> the first object to be envied is the feeding breast for the infant feels that it possesses everything that he desires and that it has an unlimited flow of milk and love which it keeps for its own gratification.

For Klein, 'he' seems to be used as a quasi-generic pronoun as the infant is in a state 'prior to the firm imposition of gender roles,' to re-use Sofoulis's terms. For this quasi-gendered infant, the feeding, or good, breast is, in Biblical terms, the land flowing with milk and honey, the Promised Land, Australia Felix, whereas the non-feeding or bad breast is the dry and barren land, the Wasteland, the Desert, the interior of Australia through the eyes of European explorers and settlers (see Falkiner, 1992). The construction of the earth as rich and bountiful, especially in mining terms, has recently been employed by the Western Australian Chamber of Mines (1990, p. 1) that describes Western Australia as having been 'endowed with rich mineral resources.' Good breast indeed.

For the young infant, though, there is no distinction between the body of the mother and other external objects, so we are not in the realm of the figurative here where the Promised Land and Desert are just mere metaphors for the mother's body. No distinction has yet been made between the mother and the external world in general so the child is in a pre-metaphoric stage or state in which the body of the mother and Mother Earth are one. The two *topoi* are mapped onto each other and the relationship with one becomes the model for the relationship with the other. Not only are the mother's body and the external world mapped onto each other for the young infant, but also the changing and developing relationship between child and his/her mother becomes the model for his/her relationship with the external world. How we human beings treat the earth is modelled on how we treated our mothers.

This oneness and modelling is no more cogently described than by Marie Bonaparte (1949, p. 286) (though interestingly without acknowledging

Klein) in her well-known psychoanalytic study of the life and works of Edgar Allen Poe:

> the child at the breast knows nothing of the world: all it knows of it is the breast that gives it milk. This breast is more than something it may claim, it seems part and parcel of its own body. Thus, the mother's proximity, by degrees, develops in the child its first conceptions of the outside world, for it soon learns to know presence or absence, her yielding or withholding of the breast. Thus, to it, she is the first embodiment of that nature by which it is surrounded, whose every constituent, by degree, attaches itself to the primal figure of the mother. Later, in adult life, nature which both feeds and harshly uses man will, by a sort of regression, come to symbolize the mother upon whom, originally, that nature was modelled but, now, as an immensely magnified, eternal, infinite mother. Thus, the manner in which each of us loves nature, always reflects, more or less, our own mother-complex.

Yet this relationship not only involves the way 'nature' 'harshly uses man.' It also invariably involves the way modern 'man' harshly uses nature. In psychoanalytic terms the way modern 'man' harshly uses nature is sadistic which can be defined, as Freud did, not only as deriving pleasure from the pain of others, but also simply as setting up the subject–object distinction, and instituting a relation of mastery between subject and object. The discourses of nature that construct nature as object and a subject position of power/knowledge against it, and the industries that extract resources from nature and construct it as compliant object, both establish and enact a sadistic, subject–object relationship with nature.

The envy or desire for the good breast gives rise to what Klein (1986, p. 110) calls 'sadistic appropriation and exploration of the mother's body and of the outside world (the mother's body in an extended sense),' or Mother Earth. For Freud ontogenesis, the beginnings of the individual, recapitulates phylogenesis, the beginnings of the species. The sadistic exploration and appropriation of the body of Mother Earth can be construed in terms of the history of Western exploration and colonial appropriation. For the young infant, in Klein's (1986, p. 116) terms, this sadistic exploration and appropriation of the surfaces or the outside of the mother's body, is followed by the sadistic exploration and appropriation of the depths, or the inside of her body:

> in the very first months of the baby's existence it has sadistic impulses directed, not only against its mother's breast, but also against the inside

of her body: scooping it out, devouring the contents, destroying it by every means which sadism can suggest.

Exploration and appropriation of the surfaces of the earth is followed by exploration and appropriation below the surface; landscape by mining; Columbus by Cortez (see Todorov, 1984). For Aboriginal poet West (Gilbert 1988, p. 175; Sabbioni, Schaffer and Smith, 1998, p. 149) in a poem entitled, 'I feel the texture of her complexion with both hand and heart,' this process is a cancer:

> you rip out her heart, her spleen and liver –
> mining, digging, drilling, a cancer attacking the essence of my life.

Even standard textbooks on mining and minerals such as *Minerals and Men* [*sic!*] construct their own discourse in terms similar to those that Klein uses to describe the young infant's relation to his/her mother's body and Aboriginal poets use to describe mining's relation to Mother Earth, though, of course, uncritically:

> since before the dawn of recorded history man [*sic*] has looked to the earth for materials from which to build his shelters and to make his tools and utensils. Over the centuries this gouging and scratching at the surface to find clay, flint, bright stones, or occasional pieces of native copper evolved into a burrowing beneath the surfaces in the broadening search for mineral materials. As history has progressed the need for minerals has increased, and the search has gone on. Indeed, the passage of time has seen the use of an ever-increasing array of mineral raw materials, in ever-expanding quantities, for a multitude of purposes – materials which man recovers from the ends and depths of the earth.
> (McDivitt and Manners, 1974, p. 3)

Early mining is here figured in the sadistic terms of gouging and scratching at the surface of the earth. Later, industrial capitalist mining is figured as 'burrowing' beneath the surface like a mole and 'recovering' what would otherwise be 'lost' in the 'depths' of Mother Earth. Elsewhere mining is figured as 'winning' and 'bringing to fruition' 'the potential riches that lie buried' (see Trigger 1997, pp. 165, 167). More 'environmentally friendly' metaphors are needed than these for mining, such as eating gratefully at the table of Mother Earth and appreciating sensually the goods she generously gives rather than greedily gorging on ore bodies and resource commodities.

For Klein (1986, p. 177), the sadistic impulse of the young infant to appropriate the good things in the depths of his mother's body is described as 'oral–sadistic impulses to rob the mother's body of its good contents.' Discourses of mining have also seen mining as stealing the good contents of the earth. This is no more graphically illustrated than on the cover of a booklet produced by the Australian Mining Industry Council entitled *Mining . . . and the Environment* (Hore-Lacy, 1976) (note the order of priority (why not *The Environment and Mining*?) and the ellipses indicating deferral and delay as if 'the environment' were an afterthought). The cover depicts the good contents of the earth in an image of sparkling and shiny goodies at the bottom of a deep, penetrating shaft. Mining is figured in the illustration as a penetration of the surface of the earth through a discrete, and discreet, hole that leaves untouched the surrounds. Much mining, however, does not in fact take place through this confined penetration but by scratching and gouging the surface of the earth through 'strip mining,' or in the words of Aboriginal poet Elizabeth Brown (Gilbert, 1988, p. 184) in a poem entitled, 'Spiritual Land,' 'Hunger for money, stripped the land/mined the Earth.' This can readily be seen as a kind of phallic fantasy of mining/rape, of 'shafting' the earth in two senses.

For Klein, this sadistic impulse of the young infant to rob the mother of her good contents is coupled to and followed by a sadistic impulse to expel the bad things of his own body into her. Klein (1986, p. 177) refers to these as the young infant's 'anal–sadistic impulses to put his excrements into her.' In environmental terms, the good contents of Mother Earth are robbed, 'recovered' or 'reclaimed' (see Trigger, 1997, p. 170) by mining and the bad excrements of consumption are put back into the earth by 'sanitary land-fill.' This process is no more powerfully, and protestingly, put than in the words of Aboriginal poet Noonuccal (Gilbert, 1988, p. 101):

The miner rapes
The heart of earth
With his violent spade.
Stealing, bottling her black blood
For the sake of greedy trade.
On his metal throne of destruction,
He labours away with a will,
Piling the mountainous minerals high
With giant tool and iron drill.

In his greedy lust for power,
He destroys old nature's will.
For the sake of the filthy dollar,
He dirties the nest he builds.

The throne here is ambiguously the seat of regal power and the toilet pan in the waste closet. Whereas soil erosion 'rapes' the surface of the earth, mining 'rapes' its depths. Mineral raw–materials are extracted, processed, munched over, transformed into energy and commodities which are bought and sold, consumed and used, ingested and digested, excreted and discarded into 'sanitary land-fills' and elsewhere in the earth-household, including the atmosphere. Mining scoops out the earth and creates hollow places; sanitary landfill finds hollow places in the earth and fills them up. Invariably these hollow places have been wetlands. An all too familiar scene in Australia and the United States has been of what was once a wetland, but is now a wasteland full of rusting car bodies, bald tyres, superseded whitegoods and sundry other household rubbish, the detritus of capitalist production and consumption.[1]

These oral–sadistic and anal–sadistic impulses arise for Klein (1986, p. 183) not only out of a desire to sadistically hurt or harm the mother and to derive pleasure from that, but also out of a desire to master and own her. In drawing this distinction between the *oral*–sadistic impulses to 'suck dry, bite up, scoop out and rob the mother's body of its good contents' and the *anal*–sadistic impulses to 'expel dangerous substances (excrements) out of the self and into the mother,' Klein (1986, p. 183) goes on to argue that these dangerous substances and bad parts of the self are:

> meant not only to injure but also to control and to take possession of the object. In so far as the mother comes to contain the bad part of the self, she is not felt to be a separate individual but is felt to be the bad self. Much of the hatred against parts of the self is now directed towards the mother.

In environmental terms, insofar as Mother Earth comes to contain excrement, she is not felt to be a separate entity, but is felt to be the bad self. Much of the hatred against parts of the self is now directed towards Mother Earth. Insofar as wetlands come to contain rubbish and other excrement, they are not felt to be separate entities. They become environmental 'dunny holes' into which waste is dumped or flows (see McComb and Lake, 1990, p. 12). Much of the hatred against parts of the self is now directed towards wetlands.

For Klein (1986, pp. 212–213) oral–sadistic impulses can be seen as greed and anal–sadistic impulses as envy. She defines greed as:

> an impetuous and insatiable craving, exceeding what the subject needs and what the object can and wishes to give. At the unconscious level, greed aims primarily at completely scooping out, sucking dry and devouring the breast, that is to say, its aim is destructive introjection; whereas envy not only aims at robbing in this way, but also at putting badness, primarily bad excrements and bad parts of the self, into the mother – first of all into her breast – in order to spoil and destroy her; in the deepest sense this means destroying her creativeness. This process I have defined . . . as a destructive aspect of projective identification.

Greed is voracious and destructive mining, and envy both this and shitting on the earth and attempting to destroy its creativeness. Besides Noonuccal's protestation about mining as a greedy trade and the miner's greedy lust for power, other Aboriginal poets, such as Russell (Gilbert, 1988, p. 3) have also protested that 'the Company kills with greedy mirth.' Unlike Michael Douglas's yuppie entrepreneur Gordon Gecko in Oliver Stone's film *Wall Street* for whom 'greed is good,' for Klein greed is gluttony, or more precisely, cannibalistic and destructive gluttony, as it is for the Aboriginal people of Australia.

Minerals and Men unapologetically constructs its own discourse in similar oral–sadistic terms – albeit unwittingly and uncritically:

> the world's appetite for minerals is great, and is steadily increasing . . . This gargantuan appetite for raw materials, and the questionable ability of the earth to continue satisfying it, provides the starting point for any consideration of minerals. The possible exhaustion of useful mineral supplies has long been a matter of concern for thinking man.
>
> (McDivitt and Manners, 1974, p. 4)

Here greed is writ large in all its oral sadism, particularly in the use of the adjective 'gargantuan' (see also Trigger, 1997, p. 166). Drawing on chapters 7 and 44 of François Rabelais's *Gargantua*, Bakhtin (1968, pp. 459–460) has traced how the word 'gargantua' 'in spanish . . . means the throat. The Provencal tongue has the word "gargantuan" meaning a glutton.' He goes on to argue that 'gargantua' 'symbolize[s] the gullet, not as a neutral anatomical term but as an abusive-laudatory image: gluttony, swallowing, devouring, banqueting. This is the gaping mouth, the grave-womb, swallowing and generating.' Fears about birth and the mother's body are displaced into images of oral gluttony.

Although the gargantuan gluttonous like Rabelais's Gargantua consume vast quantities, they do not necessarily become obese as a result of their gluttony. The gluttonous swallow dead objects external to themselves, whereas for Jean Baudrillard (1990, p. 32) the obese may be thought of as having 'swallowed their own dead bodies while still alive.' The gluttonous do not show any sign of their gluttony with their bodies whereas the obese show with the expansiveness of their own bodies the sign of their auto-necrophagy.

Envy for the creativeness of the mother's body and of Mother Earth is ultimately envy of the mother's ability to produce children (womb envy) and milk (breast envy) and of the earth to produce life and raw materials. The young infant is unable to create anything new; all s/he does is transform food into excrement as an eating–shitting factory. For Klein (1986, p. 219), 'excessive envy of the breast is likely to extend to all feminine attributes, in particular to the woman's capacity to bear children. At bottom, envy is directed against creativeness.' Industrial capitalism does not create, nor bring into being out of nothing (*ex nihilo*, like God). Rather, it transmutes prior existing matter, reshaping raw materials into 'commodities' and commodities into consumer 'goods,' sublimating solid matter into gaseous air. Arguably there are no economic modes of production, only modes of transmutation. There is, however, a biological mode of production and it is the reproduction of humans by women.

The envy of the breast, this desire for the creativeness of the mother's body, gives rise to what Klein (1986, p. 74) calls 'the femininity complex' in males in which 'the vagina and the breasts, the fountain of milk . . . are coveted as organs of receptivity and bounty,' what could simply be called 'womb envy.' These involve firm gender roles in which the boy/son may develop a complex about the creativeness of his mother's body and of Mother Earth and continues to direct envy, greed and sadism towards it/her, whereas in Kleinian terms the girl/daughter may convey gratitude towards it/her.

In terms of mining as it is currently construed, the rich and bountiful insides of the earth are coveted as 'organs' which receive and create. This covetousness, one of the seven deadly sins in medieval Christianity and sometimes seen as the basis for all the others, gives rise to technologies of 'production,' to simulated organs, 'Bachelor Machines for Bachelor Births,'[2] which receive raw materials and transmute them into consumer goods.

In these terms, envy evades obesity that Baudrillard (1990, p. 27) describes as 'a foetal obesity, primal and placental: as if they were pregnant with their own bodies but could not be delivered of them.' Unlike the gluttonous who swallow objects besides themselves and envy the creativity of the mother's body and the fecundity of Mother Earth, the obese swallow themselves and become, as it were, pregnant with, but unable to be delivered of, themselves. The gluttonous envy motherhood, whereas the obese take it over into themselves.

Gluttonous envy of the creativeness of the mother's body is associated for Klein with the formation of the superego – the internalized principle of the Law of the Father. Klein (1986, pp. 50–51) argues that 'the internalization of an injured and therefore dreaded breast on the one hand, and of a satisfying and helpful breast on the other is the core of the superego.' It is the core of the superego because it involves a turning away from the mother and her body and a turning towards the father and the Law. This is effected through a splitting in not only the mother's body into the good and bad breast, but also in the infant him/herself. Klein (1986, p. 181) argues that 'the ego is incapable of splitting the object – internal and external – without a corresponding splitting taking place within the ego.' The ego is split between the superego, the internalization of the Law of the Father, and the id, the site of repressed desire for the creativeness of the mother's body.

In this process of internalization, of gluttony and obesity, the ego gives birth to itself as a split ego. Indeed, it gives birth to itself as an infantile ego which it remains as Norman O. Brown argues:

> through the institutionalisation of the superego the parents [including the mother insofar as she is complicit with the Law of the Father] are internalized and man finally succeeds in becoming father of himself, but at the cost of *becoming his own child and keeping his ego infantile.*
>
> (cited by Eagleton, 1990, p. 272; my emphasis)

Klein located the formation of the superego far earlier than Freud did in the period when the young infant desires to scoop out and devour the contents of his or her mother's body. In this process, the young infant demonstrates envy for the creativeness of his/her mother's body and is able to give birth to him/herself as an ego but at the price of keeping that ego infantile. Thus, by implication and analogy, the desire to scoop out and devour the good contents of Mother Earth is, in Kleinian terms, infantile.

As this ego is infantile it is not strictly precise to describe the system that it founds as 'patriarchal capitalism.' Although it is certainly male-dominated, it is not dominated by the fathers, but by the sons. Klaus Theweleit (1987, 1989), in his suggestive and sweeping two-volume study of *Male Fantasies*, prefers the term 'filiarchal,' the rule of the sons. Gayle Rubin (1975, p. 168) has proposed that the term patriarchy be reserved for

Old Testament families of the pastoral nomad type in which the father did rule. All post-pastoralist social arrangements (such as agricultural and capitalist ones) would be by implication filiarchal. Yet, as I have tried to show using Klein's work, it is not just sons *per se* who rule industrial capitalism, but infantile sons, so if it were not such a mouthful and so hard swallow, it would be more precise to talk about infantile filiarchal capitalism, instead of patriarchal capitalism. In this system infantile sons sadistically devour the contents of Mother Earth and sadistically excrete their waste into it/her, not realizing, or more precisely repressing the realization, that the earth sustains their very life and being, that its resources are not inexhaustible, that she is not an indulgent and forgiving Mother who will allow herself to be abused indefinitely, and that there are limits to her resources and to her ability to absorb and hide his excrements, all too obvious in these days of widespread air, land and water pollution.

In a critical inversion of the terms and in a critique of industrial capitalism Émile Zola (1954, pp. 21, 39) figured the mine as an oral–sadistic monster. In *Germinal*, first published in 1885, instead of the miner eating the earth, the mine eats miners. The mine pit is figured as 'evil-looking, a voracious beast crouching ready to devour the world' that soon 'gulped down men in mouthfuls.' The mine, not the miner, is a greedy, oral sadistic monster like the steam saws that ate up the forests, the steam dredgers that ate up wetlands and the steam trains that ate up the bush (see Giblett, 2011, chapter 6). The pit is figured later as a greedy and gluttonous mouth: 'the cages sild up and down stealthily like beasts of the night, and went on swallowing men as though the pit were a mouth gulping them down' (Zola, 1954, p. 44).

The mine consumes 'men' (though also children) and mining is figured as 'burrowing' beneath the surface as it is in *Minerals and Men*: 'the greedy pit had swallowed its daily ration of men; nearly seven hundred of them were now toiling in this immense ant-hill, burrowing in the earth, riddling it with holes like old, worm-eaten wood' (Zola, 1954, p. 49). Burrowing begins with shafting and in Zola's *Germinal* the shaft is figured in oral–sadistic terms as eating 'men' (though the 'men' include young girls and boys): 'the shaft went on with its meal for half an hour, gulping men down more or less greedily according to the depth of the level they were bound for; but it never stopped, for the hunger of this gigantic maw could swallow up a whole people' (Zola, 1954, p. 40). Yet it is a maw created and produced by 'men.' It is the greedy, oral–sadistic monster of industrial capitalism with its greedy, oral–sadistic machines.

Similar sentiments were voiced earlier in Australia. On his visit to Australia in 1871 Anthony Trollope (1987, *I*, p. 61; see also *II*, p. 213) described how a quartz-crushing machine 'goes on day and night eating up the rock which is dragged forth [kicking and screaming, or mute and inarticulate?] from the bowels of the earth' and how 'the noisy monster continued his voracious meals without cessation.' Like the steam trains that ate up the bush, the steam dredgers that devoured wetlands, the steam saws that chewed up forests, the mines that eat up men, women and children and the miners that consume the earth, the crushing machine is an oral–sadistic monster that eats up rock.

These monsters were the brain-child of monstrous parents as D. H. Lawrence (1977, p. 124) put it: 'the idea, the IDEA, that fixed gorgon monster, and the IDEAL, that great stationery engine, these two gods-of-the-machine have been busy destroying all *natural* reciprocity and *natural circuits*, for centuries.' The copulation, or articulation, of these two monsters/machines created the oral sadistic machines of industrial capitalism that devoured everything and produced the wasteland of trench warfare that Benjamin (1999, pp. 318–319) saw:

> it should be said as bitterly as possible: in the face of 'this landscape of total mobilisation,' the German feeling for nature has had an undreamed-of upsurge. The pioneers of peace, who settle nature in so sensuous a manner, were evacuated from these landscapes, and as far as anyone could see over the edge of the trench, the surroundings had become the terrain of German Idealism; every shell crater had become a problem; every wire entanglement an antinomy; every barb a definition; every explosion a thesis; by day, the sky was the cosmic interior of the steel helmet, and at night, the moral law above. Etching the landscape with flaming banners and trenches, technology wanted to recreate the heroic features of German idealism. It went astray. What it considered heroic were the features of Hippocrates, the features of death. Deeply imbued with its own depravity, technology gave shape to the apocalyptic face of nature and reduced nature to silence – even though this technology had the power to give nature its voice.[3]

Industrial technology reduced nature to the mined moonscape, the town dump and the refuse-clogged creek, the landscape of the trench war that modern industrial 'man' has declared and fought against nature.

Towards gratitude for generosity

Rather than enviously and sadistically devouring the good contents of the earth, gratitude should be given in response to the generosity of the earth. Unlike envy that has a desire only for gratification, gratitude has a desire for complementarity and mutuality that may give rise to love. Klein (1986, pp. 215–216) argues that:

> a full gratification at the breast means that the infant feels he has received from his loved object a unique gift, which he wants to keep. This is the basis of gratitude. Gratitude includes belief in good objects and trust in them. It includes also the ability to assimilate the loved object – not only as a source of food – and to loved it without envy interfering. The more often this gift is fully accepted, the more often the feeling of enjoyment and gratitude – implying the wish to return pleasure – is experienced. Gratitude is closely bound up with generosity.

Presumably, on the other hand, by implication, envy is closely bound up with possessiveness and parsimony. In terms of mining, this would require, not just some sort of 'land-care ethic,' certainly not as an externally imposed code, but learning to be grateful to the earth and loving it. Many mining companies are good corporate citizens. They have programmes of environmental rehabilitation and restoration of their own sites, or programmes promoting land care and bush regeneration, or programmes nurturing cross-cultural understanding of indigenous culture, but how many have programmes promoting gratitude and generosity to the earth amongst its employees, its customers and the consumers of commodities made from its raw materials?

Along similar lines in the 1920s Benjamin (1979, p. 60, 1996, p. 455) warned that:

> In accepting what we receive so abundantly from nature we should guard against a gesture of avarice. For we are able to make Mother Earth no gift of our own. It is therefore fitting to show respect in taking, by returning a part of all we receive before laying hands on our share. This respect is expressed in the ancient custom of the libation.

How many mining companies make annual libations or perform rituals to express gratitude to the earth for its generosity in giving ore, jobs, profits to mining companies and dividends to shareholders? How many mining companies have an annual barbeque or picnic on World Environment Day or on Mother's Day (Earth Mother's Day?) at which, say, 'a slab of tinnies' (Australian slang for a carton of 24 or 30 aluminium cans of beer) is buried to give back a token of what has been taken from the earth? A block of concrete commemorating the event with a suitable inscription on it expressing gratitude for generosity placed over the buried booty would also help to prevent theft by the greedy and ungrateful. This may sound like a trivial and tokenistic gesture when a grand political strategy is required but its pragmatic and tactical reciprocity at the level of everyday life may help to develop mutuality with the earth. It is at this popular cultural level that conservationism and green politics need to engage with industrial workers, their families and friends.

Without such acts of libation the consequences of greed and gluttony are disastrous. Benjamin (1979, p. 60, 1996, p. 455) went on to forewarn that:

> If society has so degenerated through necessity and greed that it can now receive the gifts of nature only rapaciously, that it snatches the fruit unripe from the trees in order to sell it most profitably, and is compelled to empty each dish in its determination to have enough, the earth will be impoverished and the land yield bad harvests.

Taking the good things of the earth sadistically without returning a portion in gratitude results in bad things being given back in return.

Rather than discoursing about the earth as a passive and compliant object, a new way of talking about mining is needed that will recognize and respect the earth as an active, equal and different agent and subject and then interact accordingly in complementarity and dialogue with it. Instead of seeing the earth as something out there to exploit by mining, mining needs to see the earth as its equivalent other, not its inferior object, but at least its equal in importance with which to have relations of respect and care, and even learn to love it/her. After all, the earth is our mother beyond mere metaphor. She can live without us, but we human beings cannot live.

Notes

1 For a graphic representation of such scenes see the photographs by Wayne Lawler in McComb and Lake (1990, p. 225) and by Joseph Muench in Niering (1966, pp. 164–165).
2 For metaphors of fertility and pregnancy in mining see Trigger (1997, p. 173). For 'Bachelor Machines for Bachelor Births' see Giblett (2008a, pp. 95–98, 2009, pp. 35, 78, 167–168) and Theweleit (1987, p. 315, 1989, p. 127).
3 I discuss the landscapes of world warfare in Giblett (2009, chapters 4 and 5).

References

Agricola, G. 1960. *De re Mettalica*, H. Hoover and L. Hoover, trans. New York: Dover.
Bakhtin, M. 1968. *Rabelais and His World*, H. Iswolsky, trans. Cambridge, MA: The MIT Press.

Baudrillard, J. 1990. *Fatal Strategies: Crystal Revenge*, P. Beitchman and W. Nies-luchowski, trans. New York and London: Semiotext(e) and Pluto.

Benjamin, W. 1979. One Way Street. *In*: E. Jephcott and K. Shorter, trans., *One Way Street and Other Writings*. London: New Left Books, pp. 45–104.

Benjamin, W. 1996. One Way Street. *In*: M. Bullock and M. Jennings, eds., *Selected Writings: Volume 1, 1913–1926*, Cambridge, MA: The Belknap Press of Harvard University Press, pp. 444–488.

Benjamin, W. 1999. Theories of German Fascism. *In:* M. Jennings, H. Eiland and G. Smith, eds., *Selected Writings: Volume 2, 1927–1934*. Cambridge, MA: The Belknap Press of Harvard University Press, pp. 312–321.

Bonaparte, M. 1949. *The Life and Works of Edgar Allan Poe: A Psycho-Analytic Interpretation*, J. Rodker, trans. London: Imago.

Boyle, T. 1987. *World's End*. New York: Viking Press, Penguin.

The Chamber of Mines and Energy of Western Australia (Inc.). 1990. *Land Access for Mineral Exploration: The Way Ahead*. Perth: The Chamber of Mines and Energy of Western Australia (Inc.).

Conley, V. 1997. *Ecopolitics: The Environment in Poststructuralist Thought*. London and New York: Routledge.

Douglas, M. 1966. *Purity and Danger: An Analysis of the Concepts of Pollution and Taboo*. London: Routledge.

Eagleton, T. 1990. *The Ideology of the Aesthetic*. Oxford: Basil Blackwell.

Eliade, M. 1971. *The Forge and the Crucible*, S. Corrin, trans. New York: Harper and Row.

Falkiner, S. 1992. *Wilderness: The Writer's Landscape*. East Roseville: Simon and Schuster.

Freud, S. 1975. Findings, Ideas, Problems. *In: The Standard Edition of the Complete Psychological Works of Sigmund Freud, Volume XXIII*. London: Hogarth, pp. 299–300.

Giblett, R. 2008a. *The Body of Nature and Culture*. Basingstoke: Palgrave Macmillan.

Giblett, R. 2008b. *Sublime Communication Technologies*. Basingstoke: Palgrave Macmillan.

Giblett, R. 2009. *Landscapes of Culture and Nature*. Basingstoke: Palgrave Macmillan.

Giblett, R. 2011. *People and Places of Nature and Culture*. Bristol: Intellect Books.

Gilbert, K. 1988., ed. *Inside Black Australia: An Anthology of Aboriginal Poetry*. Ringwood, VIC: Penguin.

Griffin, S. 1978. *Woman and Nature: The Roaring Inside Her*. New York: Harper and Row.

Hore-Lacy, I. 1976. *Mining . . . and the Environment*. Australian Mining Industry Council.

Jacks, G. and R. Whyte. 1939. *The Rape of the Earth: A World Survey of Soil Erosion*. London: Faber and Faber.

Klein, M. 1986. *The Selected Melanie Klein*, J. Mitchell, ed. Harmondsworth: Penguin.

Lawrence, D. 1977. *Studies in Classic American Literature*. Harmondsworth: Penguin.

Leopold, A. 1991. Land Pathology. *In:* S. Flader and J. Callicott, eds., *The River of the Mother of God and Other Essays*. Madison: University of Wisconsin Press, pp. 212–217.

Leopold, L., ed. 1972. *Round River: From the Journals of Aldo Leopold*. Oxford: Oxford University Press.

McComb, A. and S. Lake. 1990. *Australian Wetlands*. North Ryde: Angus and Robertson.

McDivitt, J. and G. Manners. 1974. *Minerals and Men: An Exploration of Minerals and Metals, Including Some of the Major Problems that are Posed*, revised and enlarged edition. Baltimore: The Johns Hopkins University Press.

Merchant, C. (1980). *The Death of Nature: Women, Ecology and the Scientific Revolution*. San Francisco: Harper and Row.

Mudrooroo. 1992. Digging the Mining Tour. *In: North West Academic Staff Seminar: Commentary for a Tour of Pilbara Mining Operations by Academic Staff from the Perth University Campuses. . .* 9–11 July.

Niering, W. 1966. *The Life of the Marsh: The North American Wetlands*. New York: McGraw Hill.

Pliny the Elder. 1991. *Natural History: A Selection*, J. Healy, trans. Harmondsworth: Penguin.

Rubin, G. 1975. The Traffic in Women: Notes on the 'Political Economy' of Sex. *In:* R. Reiter, ed., *Toward an Anthropology of Women*. New York: Monthly Review Press, pp. 157–210.

Sabbioni, J., K. Schaffer and S. Smith, eds., 1998. *Indigenous Australian Voices: A Reader*. New Brunswick, NJ: Rutgers University Press.

Santamaria, B. Nd, ?1945. *The Earth – Our Mother*. Melbourne: Araluen.

Sofia, Z. 1989. The Hyperreal and the Overworked: A Philosophical View of Metro Mania. *Praxis M, 24/Arx 1989 Journal: Metro Mania*, pp. 5–10.

Sofoulis, Z. 1983. *Alien Pre-Oedipus: Penis Breast, Cannibaleyes, Qualifying Essay, History of Consciousness*. Santa Cruz: University of California.

Sofoulis, Z. 1984. Exterminating Fetuses: Abortion, Disarmament, and the Sexo-Semiotics of Extraterrestrialism. *Diacritics*, 14(2), pp. 47–59.

Suzuki, D. 1998. *Earth Time*. St Leonards: Allen and Unwin.

Thayer, R. 1994. *Gray World, Green Heart: Technology, Nature and the Human Landscape*. New York: John Wiley.

Theweleit, K. 1987. *Male Fantasies, Volume I: Women, Floods, Bodies, History*, S. Conway, trans. Cambridge: Polity Press.

Theweleit, K. 1989. *Male Fantasies, Volume II: Male Bodies: Psychoanalyzing the White Terror*, C. Turner and E. Carter, trans. Cambridge: Polity Press.

Todorov, T. 1984. *The Conquest of America: The Question of the Other*, R. Howard, trans. New York: Harper and Row.

Trigger, D. 1997. Mining, Landscape and the Culture of Development Ideology in Australia. *Ecumene*, 4(2), pp. 161–180.

Trollope, A. 1987. *Australia: Volumes I and II*. Gloucester: Alan Sutton.

Zola, É. 1954. *Germinal*, L. Tancock, trans. London: Penguin.

6   Pastoralism and oral sadism

Mary Durack's *Kings in Grass Castles* (hereafter *Kings* for short) is a classic of Western Australian settler literature. First published in 1959, it is also a best seller having gone through eighteen printings to 1991 and is still in print. Besides selling well, it seems to be well read, or at least well borrowed, as thirty-five copies are circulating in the public library system in Western Australia.[1] Generically, *Kings* is a family chronicle (Durack, 1966, pp. 13, 17) of the founding in the 1880s of a Western Australian pastoral dynasty in the northernmost Kimberley region of the state by its patriarch, Durack's grand-father, Patrick 'Patsy' Durack. Accordingly, it is a myth of origins of the self-proclaimed royal family of the east Kimberley who may have only been 'kings in grass castles' of a 'cattle kingdom' (p. 399), but who were kings initially of a kingdom of 'one and a half million acres . . . on either side of the Ord River' (p. 231) and emperors eventually, as Durack modestly boasts, of 'a sizeable pastoral empire of six to seven million acres or roughly ten thousand square miles' (p. 379). As it is also an epic (pp. 20, 232 and 262), *Kings* has an epic hero in the person of Patrick's brother Michael 'Stumpy' Durack who makes the obligatory descent into the underworld of the east Kimberley and emerges triumphant with his masculine identity secured and the dynastic aspirations of his family vindicated.

Furthermore, *Kings* is a quest narrative in search of the Golden Fleece (or more precisely, 'the golden Kimberley savannah lands' (p. 225), 'pastoral paradise' (p. 207, also 'a cattleman's paradise' (p. 208)) and 'Promised Land' (p. 221) of the Ord River. In this combined Biblical and Classical journey Michael ('Stumpy') Durack doubles as both Jason and part Moses. He finds the Golden Fleece of the east Kimberley and returns with the news to Queensland. Although he does not personally lead the chosen few on the 'big trek' (p. 231) to the Promised Land of the east Kimberley in Western Australia through the wilderness of outback Queensland and the Northern Territory (the role of leader of the trek is later taken by his nephew and the author's father, 'Long' Michael, or 'Miguel' Durack), 'Stumpy' Michael does get to enter the Promised Land unlike his Old Testament prototype.

For good measure, a 'boys' own' (in a variety of senses) imperialist adventure story of 'the conquest of this new country' to 'make a pastoral [*sic*] empire' (p. 210) is thrown in, not to mention the occasional episode from 'some Davy Crockett serial in Australian setting' (p. 356). Finally, *Kings* combines elements of the naturalist's attention to the details of flora and fauna; the romantic's love of the beautiful, the picturesque and the sublime; and last, but not least, the pastoralist's view of the land with an eye out for waterfowl, or 'game,' and good cattle country while the other eye is kept on the weather.

Yet these elements, and the discourses, the institutionalized 'ways of seeing, saying, and doing,' from which they arise, do not coexist in blissful harmony. Rather there is a constant struggle for hegemony between them that enacts a powerful class and gender politics. In patriarchy, the romantic and the naturalist have been assigned to and associated with the female/ feminine and the pastoralist to and with the male/masculine. *Kings* is no exception to this general rule. What is exceptional about it, though, is the way these elements are combined in a single text, even in a single sentence. No doubt this combination of discourses is related to its generic hybridity and, in fact, is probably even constitutive of it.

The gender, and generic, (and gender and genre are closely related as Derrida (1980), Cate Poynton (1985, especially p. 21) and Terry Threadgold (1988, especially p. 64) have argued) politics of the natural environment is most evident when it comes to the descriptions of water–bodies, especially rivers, or 'watercourses' as Durack prefers, in *Kings*. In this chapter I trace the struggle between the discourses of naturalism, pastoralism and romanticism in the representation of what could be called the wetlandscape. I also explore what could be called the eco-gender and eco-generic (also in the sense of 'genus') politics of this struggle and its psychodynamics using the work of Karl Abraham in order to show how, in the driest continent on earth, it is not just any water which is valuable for settlers, but preferably water which flows permanently and is readily accessible.

The body of patriarchal capitalism desires a constant stream of good things to consume in order to produce goods, but it also thereby produces bads. Patriarchal pastoralists are driven by corporeal demands, both their own and those of their cattle and sheep, but these have been culturally constructed in orally and anally sadistic terms in whose reproduction they collude. These terms contrast strongly with those of Aboriginal peoples for whom there is what Mudrooroo/Johnson (1979, p. 70) calls 'a loving oneness of people and earth' as we shall see in the conclusion to this chapter.

The demands of the body are not free from acculturation; the body is not an ideologically neutral zone (see Giblett, 2008).

Nor is the body of the earth. Water is a good and bad thing. It is a highly ambivalent substance for settlers as Durack (1966, p. 252) points out when she refers to 'death-dealing, life-giving water.' Living water is the life-blood of the body of the living earth (see Giblett, 2008, chapter 11; 2009, chapter 11); polluted water is the death-poison for the corpse of the earth. From the pastoralist point of view, flowing and masculinized rivers are generally preferred over still and feminized wetlands, whereas from the romantic and naturalist perspective the reverse largely applies, with the notable exception of slimy bogs and sloughs. An eco-gender politics and taxonomy of the landscape, or more precisely wetlandscape, operates just as much, and as powerfully, as taxonomies of flora and fauna with their own eco-generic politics. In the conclusion to the chapter I will offer, by way of a reading of *To the Islands* by Randolph Stow and *Long Live Sandawara* by Colin Johnson (now Mudrooroo), views of the Kimberley wetlandscape which contrast with those in *Kings* and make some modest proposals for an alternative, or oppositional, way of talking about it.

Politics of water

In *Kings*, water is preferably of a certain type in a branching and descending set of distinctions and scale of preferences dividing into finer and finer detail until ultimately the taxonomy is resolved into a simple binary opposition. For a start, waters which are clean, shiny and contained are preferred over those which are dirty, slimy and extensive, or in other words, billabongs rather than bogs or sloughs; rivers or 'watercourses' which flow in prescribed channels rather than swamps which are stagnant without definite boundaries; rivers which are permanent, not temporary; permanent rivers which are accessible to stock (and so orally satisfying) and not inaccessible at the bottom of steep gorges (and so orally sadistic); all of which boils down ultimately to the privileging of the Ord River over all non-Ord waters and the binary opposition between the two. I have attempted to lay out these distinctions spatially in a chart (see Figure 6.1, p. 78). A distinctive pastoralist and patriarchal political and economic agenda for the natural environment is pursued in *Kings* which ultimately wins out over the naturalist's and romantic's view, though both these are arguably as patriarchal as the pastoralist as I try to indicate and are all aspects of the patriarchal paradigm as outlined in Giblett (2011, figure 1, chapter 1).

The worst water of all, the lowest of the low, in *Kings* is muddy, slimy water, though 'a well of stagnant water' (Durack, 1966, p. 90) is better than

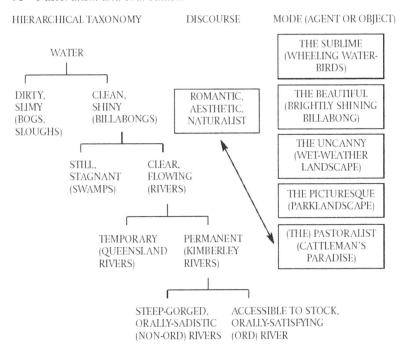

Figure 6.1 The structural process of *Kings in Grass Castles*
Note: The 'Hierarchical Taxonomy' column of this chart plots the narrative trajectory and aquatic politics of Kings and should be read from top to bottom. The 'Discourse' and 'Mode' columns plot the narrational trajectory and representational politics of Kings and can be read from top to bottom and in conjunction with the 'Hierarchical Taxonomy' column (billabongs are beautiful, bogs and sloughs are uncanny). Each pivotal moment in the narrative, each significant site in the story corresponds with a bifurcation in the hierarchical taxonomy and with a shift in mode. Each mode is couched in an appropriate discourse; each discourse is instantiated in an apposite mode. The sublime, the beautiful and the picturesque modes in the romantic, aesthetic and naturalist discourses are in tension with, and eventually subsumed beneath, pastoralist discourse. The uncanny is an aberrant, anti–romantic and counter aesthetic mode that threatens to inundate and undermine both the pastoralist and romantic discourses and to return the subject to primeval and placental slime, to the abject.

nothing when you're dying of thirst. The physical needs of the body assert themselves occasionally over aesthetic desires and the pleasures of the eye. Generally, however, slimy water is treated, not merely with disdain, but with horror.[2] It is also morally opprobrious: it is 'bad water thick with green slime' (p. 104). When 'Stumpy' Michael first lands in Cambridge Gulf, he and his men have to 'plough through the reeking mud' in which they 'floundered and sank' (p. 217). Descriptions of cattle droving in *Kings* abound in references to the 'slimy mud' (p. 248), 'sticky mud' (p. 257) and even to 'the evil slime' (p. 248) of bogs and sloughs (p. 301). This dirty, slimy water mixed with earth is beyond the pale and denigrated in odious comparison to the clear, flowing water of rivers.[3]

Stagnant, swampy water is not much better, though, than dirty, slimy water. It is subject to the utilitarian view, especially for cattle, and found to be wanting: 'the vast tracts of useless, rough range, claypan and cadjibut swamp . . . lay between the good grazing areas' (p. 355, see also p. 263). The 'good grazing areas' are ones 'fed' by rivers, though not just any old river. A contrast can be made between Durack's romantic view of rivers in her native Queensland and those in the Kimberley. Writing of 'the watercourse' on the Cooper Plains near Thylungra in a chapter entitled 'A Land Loved By Birds,' Durack describes how 'through the ragged arches of bordering coolibah and wild oranges the water shone polished bright in the setting sun' (p. 110). The brightly shining billabong with definite borders is the epitome of the beautiful in Durack's nature aesthetic.

This romantic view of an aestheticized landscape (that operates in a sterile antinomy with the pastoralist and patriarchal view and so is locked into the same logic) gives way quickly to the naturalist's desire to identify and classify the birds disturbed by the coming of 'the travellers' (though the relationship of the settlers to the land was not as fleeting as this euphemistic appellation might suggest): 'parrots and water fowl of all kind, wild geese, plumed duck, spoonbill, avocets. Flocks of teal wheeled noisily with egrets, ibises, herons and pigmy geese, while pelicans, heavily rising, flapped off in the wake of low-flying brolgas' (p. 110). These birds can all be classified as waterbirds with the exception of the parrots.

Aesthetic delight in wheeling waterbirds persists throughout the book. Indeed, wheeling waterbirds ascending into the heights, though also to some extent acrobatic, brightly coloured bush birds (mainly parrots or budgerigars), produce the state of the sublime in Durack's nature aesthetic. Yet this production of the sublime sits uneasily with the status of the waterbird's class or sub-family of 'game' when she describes how 'game was plentiful, magpie geese, whistling duck, Burdekin duck went wheeling and calling in dense clouds over the lush wet-weather landscape' (p. 260). This is one sentence which combines the romantic's natural aesthetic, especially the sublime, the naturalist's observation of individual bird species, with the pastoralist's eye on his dinner and the weather. But in the process of the sublime-producing wheeling waterbirds rising above the lush wet-weather landscape, the waterbirds are abstracted from the landscape and reduced to agents of aesthetic or culinary – in the case of 'game' – satisfaction, whereas the landscape becomes objectified as background for the wheeling waterbirds, rather than being seen as their habitat, let alone as an ecosystem. Even the term 'game' smacks of what Tim Bonyhady (2000, p. 351) calls 'class oppression under England's draconian old laws.' Objectifying land as landscape and classifying edible animals as 'game' reproduces class oppression.

The waterbirds and the landscape are not only differentiated in terms of their status as agents and objects, but also in terms of the aesthetic and other responses they evoke. Whereas the waterbirds produce a sublime pleasure bordering on pain, and the satisfaction of hunger in the case of 'game,' the land arouses a horrifying desire: 'here now was the lush, tropical north that returning drovers spoke of with mixed repugnance and fascination' (Durack, 1966, p. 260). The doubling of repugnance and fascination is a precise definition of the Freudian concept of the uncanny which, Sofoulis (1988) argues, is the obverse of the sublime (as we saw in chapter 1). Fascination and repugnance were ambivalent feelings found by Freud to be aroused in men by the sight of female genitalia and described by him in his essay on the uncanny (as we also saw in chapter 1). The uncanny wet-weather wetlandscape is the womb of the tropics from which new life springs.

The combination of the sublime and uncanny here is an aesthetic of both visual pleasure and oral surfeit, of waterbirds ascending in formless profusion and of cloying taste to the point of profligate excess. 'Lush' can refer to the tender and juicy, orally satisfying qualities of luxuriant grass. It also has connotations of sexual attractiveness and excessive drinking. Generally the overall image created is that of a blowsy, slightly tipsy, middle-aged outback mother who is both sexually fascinating and physically repugnant to the randy drovers.

Lush pasture in general is the object of desire and the end of the quest in *Kings*, but in the wet season the pasture is too lush provoking repugnance and fascination rather than giving satisfaction. The ideal pasture, satisfying both orally and aesthetically, is that which 'sprang sweet and succulent on the *parched* plains' (Durack, 1966, p. 105, my emphasis), almost a contradiction in terms and nearly an impossible object. When it grows lush on the *drenched* plains in 'the wet,' however, it is an object of fascination and repugnance.

The description of sublime-producing, wheeling waterbirds culminates later with the billabong where 'thousands of wild whistling duck rose from among the reeds and lilies, and wheeled away, in serpent coils against the sunset sky' (p. 288). This is probably the only positive description of a wetland in the book and it is hardly surprising that it is of that archetypal and quintessential Anglo-Celtic Australian wetland, the billabong, mythologized in 'Waltzing Matilda.' Yet the discourses of the aesthetic and the naturalist, especially the sublime, are not allowed to persist for too long over that of the utilitarian and pastoralist, especially the culinary, for on the next page the whistling ducks have reverted to 'game' with Uncle John shooting them and boasting of bringing down twenty-four with one shot.

A similar description of a beautiful, brightly shining billabong with sublime-producing, wheeling waterbirds as well, and thus what would be the pinnacle of aesthetic delight for Durack (1983, p. 100), can be found in her novel *Keep Him My Country*: 'the billabong shone like bright enamel under a sunset sky, reflecting the wheeling birds, pale lilies and dark bordering trees.' A beautiful billabong, though, can always revert to a slimy bog, and the sublime-producing, wheeling waterbirds be replaced by swarming and sadistic predatory bush birds as occurs later in *Keep Him My Country*:

> after two light seasons the big billabong had dwindled to a fetid, shallow pool in a crazy pavement of dried mud rimmed with grey coolibahs and streaky paper barks. The water birds had flown but the crows and hawks swarmed about the worm-raddled carcasses of perished stock and tormented the living animals imprisoned in the bog.
>
> (Durack, 1983, p. 206; see also p. 254)

Crows and hawks are more like insects than birds. Indeed, they are implicitly not living things and they are certainly not edible, or at least they should not be eaten in accordance with the Biblical injunction of Mosaic law that 'every swarming thing that swarms upon the earth is an abomination; it shall not be eaten' (Leviticus 11:41).

Swarming creatures, Douglas (1966, p. 56) has commented, are:

> Both those that teem in the waters and those that swarm on the ground. Whether we call it teeming, trailing, creeping or swarming, it is an interminable form of movement. . . 'swarming' which is not a mode of propulsion proper to any particular element, cuts across the basic classification. Swarming things are neither fish, nor flesh, nor fowl. Eels and worms inhabit water, though not as fish; reptiles go on dry land, though not as quadrupeds; some insects fly, though not as birds. There is no order in them. . . . As fish belong in the sea so worms belong in the realm of the grave with death and chaos.

For Durack, swarming bush birds are neither game to be shot nor fowl to be eaten; for her, some birds fly (and torment like insects), but do not wheel as waterbirds. The only living and edible things in this half-dead land seem to be waterbirds and cattle, a carnivorous diet.

This settler view can be contrasted with that of a visitor, Isaac Steinberg, the Jewish Territorialist, who visited the east Kimberley in 1939 to assess its suitability for a Jewish settlement. According to Leon Gettler (1993, p. 75), he had expected to find 'the dead country, the wilted Nature, the arid waste land.' Instead, he found 'the very opposite: a country that was alive, a Nature that breathed and teemed, a land peopled with all sorts of creatures.' Steinberg (1948, p. 19), though, is like Durack, as we shall see later, when he occasionally comes across 'grass so fragrant and cheerful that I could have fancied himself on some exquisitely cultivated English estate.'

In both *Kings in Grass Castles* and *Keep Him My Country* waterbirds are constantly privileged over all other birds, especially predatory bush birds, mainly on the basis that waterbirds in general produce the state of the sublime when wheeling and that 'game' presumably are orally satisfying when eaten (though there are no descriptions of the process of eating and the taste of 'game' in the book), whereas bush birds are sadistic when swarming and frustrate orally as they are inedible. Durack's taxonomy of birds is based on both aesthetic and culinary criteria with predatory bush birds being sadistic and inedible, wheeling birds producing the sublime, and 'game' being edible.

Generally the variety of waterbird species, and indeed the presence of the waterbirds themselves, is merely indexical of 'good land.' In *Kings* the settlers are described as 'ardent naturalists' (Durack, 1966, p. 116), not so much because they could identify and classify waterbirds and appreciate their colours, flight and song, but because they had learned 'to read significance in the habits and antics of birds' (p. 117). Birds are reduced to agents of the sublime when wheeling, or to mere signifiers, indeed indices, in a semiotic chain in which they either signify 'good land' in the case of waterbirds, or 'bad season' as we shall see in a moment in the case of bush birds. The romantic's and naturalist's view of waterbirds and the land gives way immediately to the pastoralist's in which 'a land loved by birds must be good land' (p. 110). Waterbirds are abstracted from their habitat and reduced to indices of good land in pastoralist terms, or if wheeling to agents of the sublime in aesthetic terms. 'Good land' is 'the pastures of a grazier's dream' (pp. 109–110), a wish-fulfilling wet daydream no doubt. The land is good, not for the birds themselves, but for cattle where goodness is equated with and reduced to the ability of the land to sustain or 'run' a certain number or 'head' of cattle per acre.

Birds in general had their pastoralist uses. The presence of waterbirds indicated good land, on the one hand as we have just seen, and the antics of bush birds pointed to bad seasons on the other:

> the blacks predicted there would be no rain that season for the chattering hordes of budgerigars that so delighted the eye with acrobatic displays, now darkening the sun like a storm cloud, now turning in a conjuror's vanishing trick on the knife edges of a million wings, were congregating too thickly about the remaining waterholes.
>
> (p. 119)

This sentence is another which combines the romantic's natural aesthetic, especially the sublime, the naturalist's observation of individual bird species, particularly their behaviour, with the pastoralist's eye on the weather. It is also one of the few positive representations of bush birds in the book.

Good land is land that could feed cattle and a bad season is a season that will not be able to feed cattle, whereas bad land is cruel and sadistic which cannot feed cattle. This distinction between good land as orally satisfying, a bad season as orally depriving and bad land as orally sadistic operates in the contrast between Queensland and Kimberley rivers:

> unlike the sprawling Queensland rivers that spread far and wide after the rains to disappear sometimes completely when the floods had run their course, the larger of these Kimberley streams had bitten deep, tortuous channels in the plains and worn towering gorges through the ranges.
>
> (p. 220)

The evanescence of Queensland rivers is unfavourable, but at least their easy-going, leisurely sprawl is in some ways preferable to the incisive oralsadism of the larger Kimberley rivers with their sharp teeth and deep throats ('gorge' is both throat and ravine).

Oral sadism

Durack anthropomorphizes the gorge rivers in the Kimberley (and the Kimberley more generally by referring to it as 'Kimberley,' ironically the name of the author's brother, one of the dedicatees of the book) by displacing onto them (by way of metaphor) the oral–sadistic qualities of tortuous biting, or more precisely, projecting on to them the fear of being bitten back by Mother Earth after having bitten into her so savagely by pastoralism (the pastoral industry, industrialized sheep and cattle grazing, not small-scale sustainable herding). The desire for and the fear of symmetry, fairness and reciprocity are important factors here. Indeed, for Karl Abraham (1966a, p. 185) 'the craving for symmetry and "fairness" . . . is often represented in the anal character,' especially the *anal*–sadistic whereby good things done to others are expected in return, whereas arguably the fear of symmetry and fairness being exercised back against oneself characterizes the *oral*–sadistic whereby bad things done to others are feared in return.

The fear of being eaten by the mother after eating her characterizes the oral–sadistic stage interposed between what Freud (1984, p. 419) calls the 'primitive oral organisation – the fear of being eaten up . . . by the father' and the 'anal–sadistic phase – the wish to be eaten by the father.' The oral sadism enacted in *Kings* is not necessarily symptomatic of any psychopathology on Durack's part personally (and I am not implying, suggesting or diagnosing any), but it is symptomatic of what could be called a cultural psychogeopathology in which there is no hard and fast divide between the normal and the pathological but more of a continuum between them. In Derrida's (1977, p. 96) terms, I am 'putting the text on the couch,' analysing, in Pierre Macherey's (1978, p. 92) words, 'the unconscious of the work (not of the author)' and getting it to speak its repressed by free association (though for Kristeva (1984, pp. 160–161) 'the text has no unconscious'). This 'talking cure,' though, is not designed to make the symptom disappear (as Freud believed it would for the analysand) from the text or from culture, but to speak the cultural symptom which figures the (Western Australian) environment in psychopathological terms (as we saw in chapter 4). In the conclusion to this chapter, I offer some alternative, or oppositional, ways to the psychogeopathological way of talking about the Kimberley (and Western Australian) wetlandscape.

Kings can be read as a symptom of a cultural pscyhogeopathology as it includes and represents what Leopold (1991, p. 217) calls 'a land pathology' in the 'collective organism of land and society.' As Leopold goes on to point out and as we saw with mining in the previous chapter, a pathology is indicated by 'self-accelerating rather than self-compensating departures from normal functioning.' *Kings* is, amongst other things, a history of pastoralism in Australia which plots the self-acceleration of the industry in the 50 years from *circa* 1850 to 1900 and the consequent departure of 'vast tracts' of land from their normal, Aboriginal functioning over the previous 50 000 years at least, 1 000 times longer.

The growth of the Australian pastoral industry constitutes land pathology if there ever were one that manifests itself in the cultural symptom of the textual trope, such as metaphor. The trope is the symptom that manifests the cultural repressed through displacement and sublimation. If, as that ostensibly arch anti-Freudian Vladimir Nabokov (1971, p. 328) suggests, 'tropes are the dreams of speech,' and if, as Freud (1976, p. 769) maintains, 'the interpretation of dreams is the royal road to the unconscious activities of the mind,' then the interpretation of tropes is therefore the royal road to the unconscious activities of speech. By reversing the processes of displacement and sublimation, the unconscious conditions of possibility of the trope can be analysed and its cultural psychogeopathology allayed, and even an alternative, or oppositional, means of meaning-making created, or at least intimated.

In Karl Abraham's psychoanalytic terms, the love of observing nature in *Kings*, such as is exemplified in bird-watching, would be seen as the sublimation of repressed desires for oral satisfaction. He suggests that:

> the displacement of the infantile pleasure in sucking to the intellectual sphere is of great practical significance. Curiosity and the pleasure in observing receive important reinforcements from this source, and this not only in childhood, but also during the subject's whole life. In persons with a special inclination for observing Nature, and for many branches of scientific investigation, psychoanalysis shows a close connection between those impulses and repressed oral desires.
>
> (Abraham, 1966b, pp. 162–163)

Observing masters objects at a distance and reduces them to passivity whereas oral satisfaction, unlike oral sadism, entails immediacy and generosity between self and other. Indeed, for Abraham,

> the act of sucking is one of incorporation, but one which does not put an end to the existence of the object. The child is not yet able to distinguish between its own self and the external object. There is yet no differentiation made between the sucking child and the suckling breast.
>
> (Abraham, 1965, p. 450)

Abraham distinguishes the earlier orally satisfying stage of the overall oral phase from the later orally sadistic stage in which 'the individual incorporates the object and so destroys it' (Abraham, 1965, p. 451). The reciprocal and mutual relationship between self and other has been taken over and superseded by the masterly and sadistic distinction between subject and object. These processes can be seen to operate in pastoralism that separates itself from the external object of the land, incorporates it orally by sheep and cattle grazing on it, and so generally destroys it. By and large, pastoralism does not operate in an environmentally sustainable way.

Pastoralism separates itself off from the land in *Kings* and sets up a sadistic subject-object relationship with it. Visual observation is dominant over oral satisfaction, the eyes over the mouth, the sense of sight over the sense of taste. Some early settlers demonstrated 'a taste for the land' (Durack, 1966, p. 207), but they are considered naïve to do so and the infantile, orally fixated cattle 'nuzzled and sucked' (p. 248), like breast-feeding babies, slimy water when nothing else was available. But what else could be expected of 'dumb animals'?! The Duracks, though, distinguish themselves from the other early settlers, and from cattle of course, by ostensibly eschewing such infantile oral pleasures and avowing adult visual pleasures.

Kings abounds in references to watching, observing, inspecting, surveying, taking 'a bird's eye view' (p. 243), not as an identification, or even empathy with the bird, but as an appropriation of the bird's point of view in order to 'look down' (p. 227) on and master the land from above. These sublimations of the oral into the visual mark a shift from oral sadism to anal sadism, from the fear of being eaten by (the) mother (earth), to what Abraham (1966a, p. 180) calls 'the subject's pleasure in looking at his [*sic*] own possessions.' It also marks a shift from the realm of the mother to that of the father, from the left–hand to the right–hand paradigm of Giblett (2011, figure 1, chapter 1).

The inspection of the land in *Kings* often has patriarchal romantic and reproductive connotations when, for example, 'the Kimberley district looked promising . . . but . . . there was a tendency with surveyor–explorers to fall in love on sight with country they discovered if it was in any way fertile' (Durack, 1966, p. 207). The reproductive metaphor is carried through into references to 'vast open plains heavy with pasture' (p. 208), like the patriarchal stereotype of a woman 'heavy with child,' though early reports of the land's 'fertility and abundance' had deceived many naïve early settlers for 'this was after all a hard land . . ., a remote and lonely land of long, dry winters and wet tropical summers' (p. 229). The bad, hard land is figured as a kind of dried-up spinster aunt, rather than as fecund Mother Earth.[4] However, the Durack pastoralist empire on both sides of the Ord was 'a vast fertile tract of river frontage' (p. 356). The Duracks may have only been 'kings in grass castles,' but they were kings of the king of Kimberley watercourses. There is more than a modicum of sadism implicitly exercised here against those who were less fortunate and well-off than the Duracks.

The pastoral conquest of the country is not only seen in sadistic terms, but also in masculinist sexual terms as 'the opening up of new and untried country' (p. 355) with its 'virgin pastures' (p. 20) when 'Stumpy' Durack 'surveys the lay of the land' (p. 222): 'far below stretched the golden Kimberley savannah lands, cut through by green ribbons of timbered gullies and creeks' (p. 225). The settler view of the land as 'virgin' territory ready for deflowering by phallic heroes is a cliché of explorer's journals (see Strang 1997, pp. 25–126). The good, soft land is figured, and fantasized, as a passively supine female body laid open to and decorated for the penetrating gaze of the epic hero as it was for the romantic poet William Wordsworth. To cap it off, inevitably there is the obligatory reference to the 'whiteman's penetration in this lonely land' (Durack, 1966, p. 227; see also p. 103) with its obvious overtones of rape.

The desire to taste and ingest Mother Earth literally is one that it is quickly repressed in Western childhood, and this desire and its repression is merely symptomatic of a larger desire to know her intimately, to feed on her as one fed on the breast of one's mother, or its substitute. This desire is displaced and sublimated into the love of looking, or scopophilia, with the emphasis shifting from immediacy to distance, from the sense of taste to that of sight, from reciprocity to sadism. The naturalist's desire to observe (and to identify and classify, and so to master) is, then, as equally masculine and sadistic as the pastoralist's desire to possess (and to own as a king of the king of Kimberley watercourses and to rule albeit from 'grass castles').

This repression of oral desire is borne out by the fact that streams in the Kimberley are contrasted between 'expanses of dry bed [which] alternated with deep green reaches where waters were held between high banks, creviced by centuries of wind and water, luxuriant with trees, creepers and trailing palms' (p. 220). The narrow, deep-throated, orally sadistic gorge rivers and the old, dry dug/bed of the bad breast contrasts with the deep and wide expanse of the good breast, the Ord River 'twenty chain width of water reaching out of sight' (p. 226), graphically illustrated in the photograph of Plate XXXVIII of the hardback edition (only) of *Kings in Grass Castles*.

The land by the Ord River is the land flowing with milk and honey, the land where, in Abraham's (1966b, p. 157) terms, the orally fixated or dissatisfied 'expect the mother's breast to flow for them eternally' and so obtain oral satisfaction. Queensland rivers and the other Kimberley rivers continually frustrated this expectation. The promised land of riverine water feeding lush pasture that, in turns, feeds cattle is where the good breast of Mother Earth flows eternally. The pastoralist discourse wins out over the discourses of romanticism and naturalism, the male/masculine over the female/feminine. Such is the completeness of this victory here that *Sons in the Saddle*, the sequel to *Kings*, has hardly a trace of the discourses of romanticism and naturalism.

The course of the other, non-Ord streams in the Kimberley is generally marked as tortuous. The Durack River is no exception in *Kings*:

> the river swung north, south and west on a tortuous route through plain and range, cutting through dense pandanus thickets and tattered

cadjibuts, cascading over rocky falls and into still reaches of pale blue lotus where jabiru and ibis preened and fished.

(Durack, 1966, p. 221)

The still reaches of placid and feeding maternity are contrasted with the sadistic knifing of the river cruelly twisting through gorges.

Rather than the gorges, Durack's great-uncle and his expedition were 'cheered [but not overjoyed] by the sight of open plains and abundant grasses – a wonderland of pasture and fine trees' with its 'even spread of golden grass' giving the impression of 'park land, artistically planned, a reserve of wild life . . ., an artist's paradise of scenery in the grand manner' (pp. 220–221). The romantic's appreciation for a picturesque English-style gentleman's parklandscape competes with, and here triumphs temporarily over, the cattleman's eye for good pasture; the pastoral wins out momentarily over the pastoralist.

The land itself, though, is generally reduced to the site of a quest, specifically an interior quest in two senses: a quest for 'manhood'; and a quest for the Ord River. Both quests are undertaken by journeying into 'the Kimberley hinterland' (p. 86; also 'the lonely hinterland' (p. 307)) beginning at 'the mouth of the Ord River' (pp. 217–219),[5] or at what was supposed was its 'mouth,' and proceeding inside it only to find other, orally sadistic rivers instead, as well as 'impenetrable gorges' (p. 301). It seems as if, despite the colonization of 'vast tracts' of the surface of Mother Earth, especially of the good breast of the Ord River and despite his desire to penetrate further, the 'whiteman's penetration in this lonely land' was only into the mouth of the Ord and not down its throat. This double quest involves the obligatory descent into the underworld as part of the epic hero's journey through which he must negotiate his way successfully in order to achieve 'manhood' and the goal of his quest.

Psychodynamically, the underworld into which the epic hero descends is the female body in general and female sexuality in particular, both figured in terms of bodies of water. This journey into the interior, or hinterland, of Mother Earth via her mouth is a regal, oral insemination by the king pastoralists of 'the queen of Australian rivers' (p. 209) out of which union a patrilineal pastoral empire is born. The patriarch was later able to boast about 'this country that I brought to life' (p. 274). The patriarch views the creation of new life as a parthenogenesis that typically overlooks the role of (the) mother (earth) and the labour of women (in a variety of senses) in reproducing life. One of the ways in which *Kings* is a boys' own story is that women, especially Aboriginal women, and their labour, are largely absent from it.[6]

The attainment of the object of the quest is repeatedly deferred by not finding the right mouth to begin with. In fact, the epic hero was not even in the area known as the 'false mouths' of the Ord on the east side of Cambridge Gulf. The epic hero has an inverted notion of female anatomy and a strange concept of sexual reproduction because he confuses the vagina with the mouth. No doubt this inversion and confusion revolves around the *vagina dentata* and no doubt this is related to seeing the tortuous gorges as orally sadistic.

The oral sadistic fear of symmetry and reciprocity being exercised back by the mother against the self produces the fear that the mother's vagina/uterus which gave life and the mother's mouth which must give pleasure to her, like the infant's gives pleasure to it by taking sustenance, will coalesce into the *vagina dentata* which would take life back and pleasure from the infant, or the infantile epic hero. This fear gives rise to the desire for oral penetration and insemination such is both the extent, and distance, to which the orally dissatisfied displace sexuality and the kind of pre-emptive 'I'll-do-you-before-you-do-me' *modus operandi* employed by them. This displacement of sexuality to the oral even has narcissistic and incestuous overtones when one of the river mouths entered in *Kings* turns out mistakenly to be the Durack, but this River 'too was not the Ord' (p. 222). The Durack is constituted as not being the Ord, a very serious liability indeed and the ultimate binary opposition in Durack's taxonomy of waters (see Figure 6.1, p.78).

Finally, in *Kings* 'a river . . . gave every promise of being the Ord at last' (pp. 222–223). The phallic pastoralists fantasize that they are 'on a promise.' The promise is fulfilled for this is the 'Promised Land,' the title of Durack's twenty-first chapter and the fulfilment of Patsy's vision that 'the Kimberley district looked promising' (p. 207). This district is the land flowing with milk and honey, the good breast of Mother Earth, from which the questing pastoralist looking for (a) good feed for his cattle, can receive oral satisfaction unlike the orally sadistic tortuous gorge rivers/*vagina dentata* which threaten to eat him up and the dry beds/dugs of the bad breast from which he can get no satisfaction.

In this quest, the pastoralist's view of the country ultimately wins out over the romantic's and the naturalist's, the sadistic over the satisfying, the anal over the oral, the masculine over the maternal (though all the former and all the latter terms are not synonymous as I have already suggested). In finding the Ord River, 'here was the pioneer landseeker's [not the romantic's nor the naturalist's] dream-come-true' (p. 226), a wet dream in a variety of senses. In contrast with Dorothea MacKellar's 'land of droughts and flooding rains,' the Ord River country is 'this new promised land of neither drought nor flood' (p. 232).

The attainment of the object of the quest marks a further shift from the oral satisfaction (of lush pastures), through the oral sadism (of the gorge rivers, the oral desires repressed by repugnance for lush pastures in the wet season and displaced into observation, the oral dissatisfaction of the dry bed), through the anal sadism of the love of looking, finally into the anal sadism of ownership and possession. For Abraham (1966b, p. 156), 'an inordinate desire to possess . . . belong[s] to the clinical phenomena of the anal character . . . built up on the ruins of an oral erotism whose development has miscarried.' This development has miscarried (an entirely appropriate metaphor) because the object of desire (lush pasture) is found (in the wet-season) to be fascinating and repugnant, whereas previously (in the dry season) the object of desire was satisfying.

Durack writes in *Kings* about how her grandfather read about the Kimberley and thought that this was 'the country he most desired – a land of splendid rivers, fine pastures and reliable rainfall' (Durack, 1966, p. 207) and she later quotes with approval how her great-uncle found 'the country everything that could be desired, suitable for all kinds of stock' (p. 226). The desirability of the country is equated with and reduced to its suitability for stock. This desire finds satisfaction in what Abraham (1966b, p. 157) calls 'the pleasure in acquiring desired objects' (a bigger station on the accessible, permanent Ord River), rather than 'the pleasure in holding fast to existing possessions' (a smaller station in Queensland near disappearing, temporary rivers). Patriarch Patsy says of the Ord River country 'it's not a property. . ., it's a Principality' (Durack, 1966, p. 232) with its king and queen (though Grandmother Mary Durack, the author's namesake, does not rate much of a mention), princes and princesses (including 'the author' (see the photograph facing p. 209), a princess of the principality and of princessly prose).

In 'marked contrast' to the evanescent, temporary rivers of Queensland, the Ord River was 'the land of permanent water, regular rainfall and abundant pasture' (p. 233). Ironically, by a cruel twist of fate (or perhaps poetic justice), Argyle Downs Station is now even more so than ever 'a land of permanent water' as it lies beneath the waters of the artificial Lake Argyle; Argyle Downs Station is no longer temporarily 'an inland sea' (p. 252) during floods, but permanently beneath one. Perhaps the ultimate irony (or eponymous poetic justice) is that Kimberley Durack seems to have been one of the first to propose the scheme of damming the Ord (p. 400). In later life Durack (1986, pp. 65–68) appears to have had second thoughts about the damming, though, and to have become ambivalent about it to the point of penning a poem entitled 'Lament for the Drowned Country.'

'A Loving Oneness of People and Earth'

The politics of Durack's views about Kimberley rivers and wetlands can be contrasted with those in the work of two other Western Australian writers:

Stow's novel *To the Islands*, first published in 1958, the year before *Kings*, and the novel *Long Live Sandawara* by Colin Johnson (now Mudrooroo), first published in 1979, twenty years after *Kings*. Unlike *Kings* which involves a quest for the promised pastoral land, *To the Islands* centres around the desire for a quiet death. On his journey from the interior to the exterior, Stephen Heriot, the dying missionary, encounters 'a clear pool with a few lilies' (Stow, 1958, p. 170). At first he is concerned, like Durack, to identify the species of waterbirds there. He then sees the pool and its waterbirds in romanticized terms with an eye, like Durack, for the aesthetic forms of dance:

> 'Look at the birds,' Heriot said. 'Brolgas'. He pointed to where, not far from them, a great flock of grey-blue birds was gathered, and three or four of them were dancing, measured and graceful, with a flowing interplay of wide wing and thin leg. 'They're happy,' said Heriot.
>
> (Stow, 1958, p. 170)

Unlike Durack though, Heriot anthropomorphizes the waterbirds in glowing, romantic terms, rather than seeing the wetlandscape in sadistic, psychogeopathological ones.

Moving closer to the pool Heriot observes more with the eye of the amateur ornithologist and aesthetic naturalist the antics of the waterbirds:

> They came to the edge of the pool, and with a great splash and a clap of wings the ducks fled from their coming, and circled above, and above the disturbed waterhole, brown ducks and black ones, and the small delicate teal in a high outcry of whistling.
>
> (Stow, 1958, p. 171)

Heriot's observation of nature is, like that in Durack's book a sublimation of oral desire. This sublimation can be seen in the contrast between Heriot's romanticized natural aesthetic and the attitude of his Aboriginal companion, Justin, who sees the pool both as source of food and object of love. After Justin shoots a goose – an act which initially appals Heriot – he remarks that 'you love the things you kill, but you never regret killing them' (Stow, 1958, p. 172) whereas white people kill the things they love and regret doing so.

The difference between the oral sadistic fear of being eaten by the land along with the anal–sadistic desire to possess the land in *Kings* and the oral desire in *To the Islands* to use and love the wetland is characteristic of what Abraham (1966b, p. 161) calls:

> the differences in the inclination to share one's possessions with others. Generosity is frequently found as an oral–character trait. In this the

orally gratified person is identifying himself [and presumably herself as well] with the bounteous mother.

Unlike the anal sadistic craving for, and the oral sadistic fear of, fairness and symmetry, the orally satisfied values mutual reciprocity and generosity. This conclusion may smack of romanticized 'noble savagery' when it is applied to Justin and indigenes more generally, but it certainly is indicative of a different kind of relationship, oral and otherwise, with the Western Australian (wet)landscape than that enacted in *Kings*, and may be indicative of a broader cultural difference in ways of living in the natural environment, of a different corporeal politics.

These differences come out strongly in *Long Live Sandawara* in which Noorak describes how:

> his first ancestors passed across this land, leaving it intact but known. Each tree, each bush, each animal, the waterholes and soaks were named and formed into a loving oneness of people and earth. No one raped and no one pillaged; love formed the bond and the Law held firm each and every particle until
>
> (Mudrooroo/Johnson, 1979, p. 70)

the unmentionable and unthinkable happened. The whiteman came, the invaders (p. 75), with their cattle 'like an army,' the invading infantry of the cavalry cattlemen, which bawl like children and pollute the waterholes (Mudrooroo/Johnson, 1979, p. 76) killing living water. Wetlands for Aboriginal people, however, are bonded into a loving unity between them and the earth, not mythologized into beautiful billabongs, nor psychogeopathologized into useless swamps, nor sublimated into wheeling waterbirds, nor polluted by trampling cattle into slimy bogs or sloughs.

Nor later in the novel are gorge rivers orally sadistic – quite the contrary:

> the Lennard river has churned [not bitten] the wild Wandjina gorge right through the Napier range. In the wet season the Wandjina spirits send floods to pour in torrents between the cliff faces. In the dry season the water retreats into the sky and the deep Wandjina pool lies peacefully between the steep limestone breasts of the mountain range.
>
> (Mudrooroo/Johnson, 1979, p. 112)

The loving, nourishing and orally satisfying oneness of Aboriginal people with their bountiful gorge rivers, waterholes and soaks is worlds away, and cultures apart, both from the aestheticisations, observations and orally sublimated distantiations of romantic naturalism with its beautiful billabongs and sublime waterbirds, and from the cruel, lonely and orally dissatisfied mastery of sadistic pastoralism with its slimy bogs or sloughs, useless swamps, tortuous gorge rivers and plentiful plains rivers, such as the Ord River where the Duracks were once kings in their grass castles of the king of Kimberley watercourses.

Notes

1 State Library Service of Western Australia cataloguing data.
2 I discus the 'horror of the slimy' and its relation to the sublime in Giblett (1996, especially chapter 2).
3 I discuss the cross-cultural colour-coding of water, the life-blood of the earth-body, in Giblett (2009, chapter 11).
4 For further discussion see Giblett (1996).
5 I discuss the mistaken view of anatomy that places the 'mouth' of a river at what is in fact the opposite end of the alimentary canal or digestive tract in Giblett (2008, chapter 11 and 2009, chapter 11).
6 Aboriginal women in the Kununurra area in the 1990s still complained about the harsh treatment they received as domestic slaves at the hands of the Duracks (Hugh Webb, personal communication).

References

Abraham, K. 1965. The Process of Introjection in Melancholia: Two Stages of the Oral Phase in the Libido. *In:* D. Bryan and A. Strachey, trans. *Selected Papers.* London: Hogarth, pp. 442–453.

Abraham, K. 1966a. Contributions to the Theory of the Anal Character (1921). *In:* B. Lewin, ed., D. Bryan and A. Strachey, trans. *On Character and Libido Development: Six Essays.* New York: Basic Books, pp. 165–187.

Abraham, K. 1966b. The Influence of Oral Erotism on Character Formation (1924). *In:* B. Lewin, ed., D. Bryan and A. Strachey, trans. *On Character and Libido Development: Six Essays*, New York: Basic Books, pp. 151–164.

Bonyhady, T. 2000. *The Colonial Earth.* Melbourne: Miegunyah Press, Melbourne University Press.

Derrida, J. 1977. Fors: The Anglish Words of Nicolas Abraham and Maria Torok. *The Georgia Review*, 31(1), pp. 64–116.

Derrida, J. 1980. The Law of Genre/La loi du genre. *Glyph*, 7, pp. 176–232.

Douglas, M. 1966. *Purity and Danger: An Analysis of the Concepts of Pollution and Taboo.* London: Routledge.

Durack, M. 1966. *Kings in Grass Castles.* Moorebank, NSW: Corgi.

Durack, M. 1983. *Keep Him My Country.* Moorebank, N.S.W: Corgi.

Durack, M. 1986. Lament for the Drowned Country. *In:* S. Hampton and K. Llewellyn, eds., *The Penguin Book of Australian Women Poets.* Ringwood, VIC: Penguin, pp. 65–68.

Freud, S. 1976. *The Interpretation of Dreams*, Pelican Freud Library 4. Harmondsworth: Penguin.

Freud, S. 1984. *On Metapsychology: The Theory of Psychoanalysis*, Pelican Freud Library 11. Harmondsworth: Penguin.

Gettler, L. 1993. *An Unpromised Land*. South Fremantle: Fremantle Arts Centre Press.

Giblett, R. 1996. *Postmodern Wetlands: Culture, History, Ecology*. Edinburgh: Edinburgh University Press.

Giblett, R. 2008. *The Body of Nature and Culture*. Basingstoke: Palgrave Macmillan.

Giblett, R. 2009. *Landscapes of Culture and Nature*. Basingstoke: Palgrave Macmillan.

Giblett, R. 2011. *People and Places of Nature and Culture*. Bristol: Intellect Books.

Kristeva, J. 1984. *Revolution in Poetic Language*, M. Waller, trans. New York: Columbia University Press.

Leopold, A. 1991. Land Pathology. *In:* S. Flader and J. Callicott, eds., *The River of the Mother of God and Other Essays*. Madison: University of Wisconsin Press, pp. 212–217.

Macherey, P. 1978. *A Theory of Literary Production*, G. Wall, trans. London: Routledge and Kegan Paul.

Mudrooroo/Johnson, C. 1979. *Long Live Sandawara*. Melbourne: Quartet.

Nabokov, V. 1971. *Ada, or Ardor: A Family Chronicle*. Harmondsworth: Penguin.

Poynton, C. 1985. *Language and Gender: Making the Difference*. Geelong: Deakin University Press.

Sofoulis, Z. 1988. *Through the Lumen: Frankenstein and the Optics of Re-Origination*, Ph.D. Thesis, History of Consciousness, University of California, Santa Cruz.

Steinberg, I. 1948. *Australia—The Unpromised Land: In Search of a Home*. London: Gollancz.

Stow, R. 1958. *To the Islands*. Ringwood, VIC: Penguin.

Threadgold, T. 1988. Language and Gender. *Australian Feminist Studies*, 6, pp. 41–70.

7   Psycho-symbiosis and the symbiocene

Biologically humans are a community. Indeed, as Theodore Roszak (1992, p. 154) argues citing Margulis, 'all organisms are "metabolically complex communities of a multitude of tightly organized beings".' For her, Roszak (1992, p. 155) goes on to relate, 'from the symbiotic point of view, there are no "individuals" – except perhaps the bacteria. All beings are "intrinsically communities".' For nearly forty years Margulis (1998, p. 33) has been the most cogent proponent of the notion of symbiosis, 'the term coined by the German botanist Anton deBary in 1873' and taken up by Eugene Warming (1909, pp. 83–95) in the early twentieth century. Margulis (1971, p. 49; see also 1981, p. 161) defines symbiosis as 'the living together of two or more organisms in close association. To exclude the many kinds of parasitic relationships known in nature, the term is often restricted to associations that are of mutual advantage to the partners.'

Symbiosis is also one of the key concepts of bioregionalism. One of the features of the bioregional paradigm for Kirkpatrick Sale (1985, pp. 50, 112), particularly as it relates to 'society,' and presumably in relation to the natural environment, is symbiosis, or, as he defines it, 'biological interaction' and 'mutual dependence as the means of survival.' Symbiosis in biological terms operates primarily at a microbiological, interspecies level, though it has wider macrobiological pertinence between animals and plants. Sale (1985, p. 113) extends its range even further and uses it as a model for 'a successful human society' which would operate symbiotically at the macrobiological, or bioregional level, particularly when it comes to cities. Yet Sale is using symbiosis in the restricted or narrow sense of mutual benefit as all animal species (including humans) are always already in symbiosis in a broader sense with the natural environment to greater or lesser extent, with greater or lesser mutual dependency and benefit. Human beings are, whether we like it or not, in symbiosis with the oxygen-producing plants of this planet. Every breath of air we breathe re-affirms this symbiosis. As Margulis (1998, p. 5) puts it, 'we are symbionts on a symbiotic planet.'

Parasitism or symbiosis?

Parasitism can be and has been a model for a 'successful' human society which survives, however parasitically, to the detriment of other species, habitats, ecosystems and biomes. Sale wants symbiosis to be a model (even a realizable utopian model) for a human society which is mutually 'successful' or sustainable with its bioregion. Rather than being a model for or a metaphor of a successful or better human society, symbiosis is the current state of play as humans are organisms, are biological creatures. Mutualism may be a useful model for a better human society, though all appeals to nature for a model of society are at best fraught with danger as nature is a cultural construct and at worst imbued with class politics for nature is an object of capitalist exploitation. Appeals to nature are to a court whose only recourse for further appeals is to refer the case on to the higher court of culture where the case is argued (and won or lost) on cultural grounds.

A mutualistic theory of human society is all very well in theory but when it comes to putting it into practice it is another matter, especially in relation to that most parasitic of beasts or even monsters, the city. It is easy to be long on generalities and short on specifics on how the city might living mutually and not parasitically in symbiosis with its bioregion. It is easy to diagnose the parasitic ills of the city but much harder to get the city to take its mutualistic medicine. Cities, Sale (1985, p. 65) argues,

> particularly modern industrial cities, are like colonizers, grand suction systems drawing their life from everywhere in the surrounding nation, indeed the surrounding world. . . . The contemporary high-rise city, in short, is an environmental parasite as it extracts its lifeblood from elsewhere and an environmental pathogen as it sends back its wastes.

It is difficult to see how such cities might cease to be parasites on their bioregion and live mutually with it. Smaller scale, decentralized communities may be able to do so.

The modern city is founded and continues to depend on a parasitic relationship with its bioregion. Despite the parasitism of the modern city, it is still in a symbiotic relationship with its bioregion and with the earth. Perhaps, as Sale suggests, it is in a pathologically symbiotic rather than healthily symbiotic relation with the world. In Mahler's terms, it is in psychotic symbiosis rather than 'normal' symbiosis. For Mahler (1972, p. 333) 'growing up' entails a gradual growing away from the normal state of human symbiosis, of 'one-ness' with the mother.' Similarly, modernity entails a gradual growing away from the 'normal' or traditional state of human symbiosis, of 'one-ness' with the earth. Modernity is thus a pathology, a land pathology and a psychopathology, a psychogeopathology. Indigenous people's oneness with the earth is the norm from which modern people have deviated pathologically, both physiopathologically and psychopathologically.[1]

Mahler (1968, p. 6) could be described as a neo-Freudian psychoanalyst whose work on what she calls 'the symbiosis theory of the development of the human being' spans over three decades beginning in the 1950s. In this theory there are basically three phases of personality development: the normal autistic; the normal symbiotic; and the separation–individuation phases. These phases refer primarily to 'the development of object relationship,' especially with the mother and corresponding roughly to Freud's oral, anal and phallic stages.

Mahler's (1968, p. 2) theory begins from the foundation of what she calls 'that vital and basic need of the human young in his [*sic*] early months of life: symbiosis with a mother or mother substitute.' For Mahler, Pine and Bergman (1975, p. 44; see also Mahler, 1968, p. 8), normal symbiosis is the phase in which 'the infant behaves and functions as though he [*sic*] and his mother were an omnipotent system – a dual unity within one common boundary,' just as the bioregion normally is the dual unity of indigenous humans with the earth within one common boundary.

The autistic child for Mahler develops a psychotic defence against the lack of this need. The psychotic symbiotic child is thus in the terms of Mahler, Pine and Bergman (1975, p. 12) 'unable to use the mother as a real external object as a basis for developing a stable sense of separateness from, and relatedness to, the world of reality.' Similarly the psychotic city–dweller is generally unable to see the earth as separate and is unable to relate to her other than as Mother Nature in the packaged commodities of nature documentaries, national parks, processed food, tourist destinations, and so on.

For Mahler and Furer (1966, p. 559) this lack of separation in 'symbiotic child psychosis' involves 'a regression to the stage of object relationship that exists before self and other representation have been distinguished.' In other words, symbiotic psychosis entails a regression to the symbiotic state of early infancy, even to the parasitic, or perhaps more precisely, intrauterine state, in which the infant is unable to distinguish between self and (m)other. Following Helene Deutsch, Mahler (1952, p. 286) argues that 'the intrauterine, parasite–host relationship within the mother organism must be replaced in the post-natal period by the infant's being enveloped, as it were, in the extrauterine matrix of the mother's nursing care, a kind of *social symbiosis*.' Mahler (1968, p. 34) repeated the same view 16 years later. Yet it is arguable whether the intrauterine relationship is strictly parasitic as the foetus does not gain considerably at the mother's expense. It is perhaps more precisely inquilistic (see later) as the uterus shares the body of the mother usually without significant disadvantage to the mother in the short-term, but often in the long run with a prolapse and the need for surgical intervention, including a hysterectomy.

Just as the symbiotic psychotic infant is unable to distinguish between self and (m)other, so the symbiotic psychotic city–dweller is unable to distinguish between self and the earth. This regression is thus, Mahler and Furer (1966, p. 560) argue, 'an archaic defence mechanism, a restitutive attempt that, by way of the delusion of oneness with the "mothering principle," serves the function of survival.' This delusion of oneness entails delusional feelings of omnipotence so for Mahler within this sense of oneness lie the seeds of its own destruction. Later she goes on to argue with Pine and Bergman (1975, p. 45; see also Mahler, 1968, p. 9) that 'the essential feature of symbiosis is hallucinatory or delusional somatopsychic *omnipotent* fusion with the representation of the mother and, in particular, the delusion of a common boundary between two physically separate individuals.'[2] The psychotic city dweller has a delusional oneness with the mothering principle of nature, and a delusional omnipotence over it/her, through the produced and packaged commodities of the hypermarket shelf and the electronic media which serve the function of survival (and to that extent is 'successful'), but not the function of living symbiotically, sustainably and spiritually with the earth.

The symbiotic psychotic, Mahler and Furer (1966, p. 560) go on to argue, does not cling to the mother *per se*, but to 'a hypercathected, yet at the same time divitalized and deanimated concrete symbol which he [*sic*] substitutes for her – a psychotic transitional object to which he constantly resorts in stereotyped fashion,' what she also calls 'a "psychotic fetish".' The living body of the earth, nurturing and horrifying, life-giving and death-dealing becomes the dead matter of Mother Nature, an industrial resource to be extracted and exploited, a commodity to be bought and sold, produced and consumed, a bauble to be fetishized by modern communication and information technologies in advertising, documentaries and tourism.

The modalities of this relationship between subject and object give rise to what Mahler (1952, p. 292) calls 'the brittle ego of the "symbiotic psychotic child"' who experiences the world as 'hostile and threatening because it has to be met as a separate being.' The response of the symbiotic psychotic, the fragile, hard–edged ego of the city dweller, to this world is to phantasize it precisely as *not* a separate being. So much for the symbiotic psychotic. What of the normal symbiotic?

The normal symbiotic child in Mahler's sense would presumably be the isolated individualist who is constituted as subject insofar as the earth is constituted as object. These terms need to be reconstrued critically in postmodern ecological terms. The 'normal' symbiotic city dweller (if such a thing is possible) or the normal symbiotic bioregion dweller, would use the bioregion as a real external subject in her own right, as Great Goddess, for developing a stable sense of inter-subjective interaction and mutual aid with her. The normal symbiotic has developed from and cannot return to the symbiosis of early infancy.

In theorizing the normal symbiotic phase of early infancy Mahler (1968, p. 7) is quite explicit that 'the term symbiosis is borrowed from biology, where it is used to refer to a close functional association of two organisms to their mutual advantage.' Yet if there is mutual advantage in the symbiosis of early infancy it is not equal as the infant requires the mother or mother substitute to survive biologically whereas the mother does not require the infant for her to survive biologically. In biological terms the relationship is strictly commensal – benefit to one, no harm to the other. Infantile and childhood development can be seen to go through two distinct symbiotic phases: first, an intrauterine period of inquilinism where, in the words of a dictionary of biology, 'one party shares the nest or home of the other without significant disadvantage to the "owner"' in contrast to parasitism 'where one party gains considerably at the other's expense'; second, a post-natal period of commensalism 'where one party gains some benefit . . . while the other suffers no serious disadvantage' (Abercrombie, Hickman, Johnson and Thain 1990, pp. 542–543). A third stage of mutuality where both parties benefit and neither suffers would perhaps ideally be achieved and maintained in later childhood and adulthood with the proviso mentioned earlier of a possible prolapse and/or hysterectomy.

Yet rather than using the term symbiosis in a strict biological sense, Mahler, Pine and Bergman (1975, p. 44; see also Mahler, 1968, p. 9) go on to argue that:

> the term *symbiosis* in this context is a metaphor. Unlike the biological concept of symbiosis, it does not describe what actually happens in a mutually beneficial relationship between two *separate* individuals of different species. It describes that state of undifferentiation, of fusion with mother, in which the 'I' is not yet differentiated from the 'not–I' and which inside and outside are only gradually coming to be sensed as different.

Yet symbiosis in the normal symbiotic relationship could describe what actually happens in a mutually beneficial relationship between two separate individuals, or more precisely communities, of different species living in a bioregion. Symbiosis would no longer be a mere 'metaphor,' or a heuristic device or explanatory trope for something else, but a lived relationship. Rather than being in a state of fusion with the earth, humans in bioregional symbiosis would experience themselves as members of a community inter-acting in mutual benefit with other species within a common bioregion, indeed, with the whole earth, and with the whole earth considered as a living organism.

Mahler's work has been critiqued for this dubious premise of an undif-ferentiated, symbiotic union between mother and child (see Klein, 1980). In the 1980s Daniel Stern (1985, p. 10) contended bluntly that 'infants never experience a period of total self/other undifferentiation.' Analo-gously the indigene is never totally undifferentiated from or completely symbiotic with the earth. In the loving union of people and earth, Aborigi-nal people are not subsumed beneath, or swallowed up by, or completely identified with, the earth to the point of losing their own separate identity. People and earth are subjects in their own right, just as the mother is a subject in her own right. Jessica Benjamin (1990, p. 20; see also Plum-wood, 1993, pp. 154–160) picked up and developed Stern's position and argued that:

> the other whom the self meets is also a self, a subject in his or her own right . . . that other subject is different and yet alike . . . the idea of intersubjectivity reorients the conception of the psychic world from a subject's relations to its object toward a subject meeting another subject.

The earth whom the self meets is also a self, a subject in its or her own right.

Although the earth is a subject like the self, the earth is not the same as the self. The earth is different and yet alike. Jessica Benjamin (1990, p. 47) argues that:

> sameness and difference exist simultaneously in mutual recognition . . . self and other are not merged . . . the externality of the other makes one feel one is truly being 'fed,' getting nourishment from the outside, rather than supplying everything for oneself.

In mutual recognition the earth is different from and the same as people. Aboriginal people and the earth are not merged into an oceanic feeling of complete undifferentiation or loss of mutually distinct identity. The externality and recognition of the earth makes one feel one is truly being fed by nourishing terrains rather than fed by consuming land, by eating earth.

The idea of intersubjectivity reorients the conception of the psychic world away from a subject's relations to its object towards a subject meeting another subject. The earth is another subject as Jessica Benjamin (1990, p. 23) puts it in relation to the mother:

> The idea of mutual recognition is crucial to the intersubjective view . . . the mother is a subject in her own right [just as the earth is, or should be, a subject in her own right]. . . . She is external reality [the earth is external reality] – but she is rarely regarded as another subject.

The earth is rarely regarded as another subject despite its generosity, despite our lack of gratitude towards it and despite the lack of reciprocity in our relationship with it/her. Yet as Serres (1982, p. 8) puts it 'the parasitic relation is intersubjective.' The parasitic city and the parasitic modern 'citi-zen' constitutes itself as subject and its host, the earth, as subject. The psychotic city dweller, by contrast, has a hypercathected and delusional sense of oneness with the earth that denies it/her subjectivity. Despite this difference, the flow of goods between the earth and the psychotic and parasitic city dweller is one way as is the flow of bads back.

A similar imbalance pertains in the relationship between the child and its parents. Jessica Benjamin (1990, p. 14) argues that 'mutuality . . . persists in spite of the tremendous inequality of the parent–child relationship.' Mutuality persists in spite of the tremendous inequality of the earth–indigene, and the even greater inequality of the earth–modern city–dweller relationship. Modern mastery has tried to supersede traditional mutuality and to reverse the tremendous inequality of the earth–indigene relationship. Despite the inequality of the modern–earth relationship, the former is still in symbiosis with the latter.

All people are parasites on the earth to a greater or lesser extent. Serres (1982, p. 24) argues that:

> man [*sic*] is the universal parasite, everything and everyone around him is a hospitable space. Plants and animals are always his hosts; man is always necessarily their guest. Always taking, never giving. He bends the logic of exchange and of giving in his favour when he is dealing with nature as a whole. When he is dealing with his kind, he continues to do so; he wants to be the parasite of man as well.

Human beings are always the guest of the earth, other animals and plants the host, but there is a world of difference between the oral and anal sadism of mining and pastoralism and the mutual recognition and symbiosis of Aboriginal people and the earth, between the mediated relationship and interaction of the former, and the immediacy of the other.

There is also a difference between indigenes and what Serres (1995, pp. 120, 122) calls astronauts who live 'off-ground' in the extra-terrestrial world of cities: 'we have all become astronauts, completely deterritorialized. . . . Astronaut humanity is floating in space like a fetus in amniotic fluid, tied to the placenta of Mother Earth by all the nutritive passages.' Astronaut humanity is floating in the womb of the biosphere tied to the earth mothership at the mouth and the anus and bathing in the amniotic fluid of the atmosphere and the electromagnetosphere inside the skin of orbital extra-terrestrial space (see the cover of *People and Places of Nature and Culture*; Giblett, 2011). Astronaut humanity is not standing with two feet planted firmly on, and rooted in, the ground, drawing nourishment from it and its goods and giving back gratitude and respect. Astronaut humanity ingests good things from the ecosphere, digests them and then excretes bad things back into it. According to Milton Klein (1980, p. 91), Mahler's concept of symbiosis is based on 'the image of an unsevered umbilical cord.' All humanity has 'an unsevered umbilical cord' attaching it symbiotically to the earth, but astronaut humanity is attached parasitically to the earth sucking out nutrients and giving back wastes, and not giving back gratitude and care.

Astronaut humanity is a parasite who, as Lawrence Schehr puts it in his 'Translator's Introduction' to Serres (1982, p. x), 'takes without giving and weakens without killing. The parasite is also a guest, who exchanges his talk, praise and flattery for food.' The city and the 'citi-zen' is a parasite which takes from the earth without giving back anything except rubbish and weakens the earth without killing it – yet – for that would be to kill itself. The parasite cannot live without the host; the host can live without the parasite. The city and the 'citi-zen' at home or abroad is also a guest who exchanges his praise and flattery of the earth for sustenance. Perhaps more precisely, a parasite is what Serres (1982, p. 8) calls 'an abusive guest.' For Serres (1982, p. 168), 'everything begins with what I call abuse value. The first economic relation is of abuse.' Relations of use and use value are pre-economic, or certainly pre-capitalist. The agricultural, manufacturing, mining and pastoralist industries are instances of industrial capitalist land *ab*use. Serres (1995, p. 36) goes on to argue later that 'the parasite routinely confuses use and abuse. The parasite would destroy the host without realizing it.' And him or herself in the process.

Without mutual recognition humans cease to exist and the earth ceases to exist too. Jessica Benjamin (1990, p. 39) argues that:

> if we fully negate the other, that is, if we assume complete control over him [or her] and destroy his [or her] identity and will, then we have

negated ourselves as well. For then there is no one there to recognize us, no one there for us to desire.

If humans fully negate the earth, that is, if humans assume complete control over her and destroy her identity and will, then humans have negated ourselves as well. For then there is no one there to recognize us, no one there for us to desire. As Serres (1995, p. 34) puts it, 'former parasites have to become symbionts. . . . This is history's bifurcation: either death or symbiosis.' The choice is simple: either no future of death or a future of symbiosis. Margulis (1998, p. 111) concurs that 'without "the other" we do not survive.'

Mutual recognition is not a moral stricture, something that humans should do or have to do out of a sense of moral obligation. Rather it is a fact of life, or perhaps more precisely a fact for life as without it humans are dead meat. Jessica Benjamin (1990, p. 40) insists that 'mutual recognition cannot be achieved through obedience, through identification with the other's power, or through repression. It requires, finally, contact with the other.' Mutual recognition between people and earth cannot be achieved through obedience to environmental laws or to the figure of the Great Goddess, nor through identification with the Great Mother's power, nor through repression of desire.

Nor even through a natural contract along the lines proposed by Serres (1995, p. 38) that 'we must add to the exclusively social contract a natural contract of symbiosis and reciprocity.' Mutual recognition between people and earth requires contact (rather than contract) with the other, with the earth in mutual reciprocity and symbiosis. Not only seeing the earth, but also tasting (and not just eating) the earth, listening, smelling and touching it – or her. To the social and natural contracts the natural contact of symbiosis and reciprocity needs to be added.

That contact can not only be sensual but also erotic. Rather than an undifferentiated relationship with the mother, Jessica Benjamin (1990, p. 29) suggests that the best model for mutual recognition is erotic union:

> in erotic union we can experience that form of mutual recognition in which both partners lose themselves in each other without loss of self; they lose self-consciousness without loss of awareness. Thus early experiences of mutual recognition already prefigure the dynamics of erotic life.

The loving oneness of Aboriginal people and earth is an erotic union in which both partners lose themselves in each other without loss of self; losing self-consciousness without loss of awareness. This loving oneness and the dynamics of erotic life may prefigure mutual recognition between modern people and earth. Dreaming ecology is erotic ecology. The bioregional dweller is a nature lover who knows intimately his or her home-habitat in what could be called an erotic ecology involving intimacy, pleasurable play, sensual appreciation through all the senses and their creative expression in many media (see Giblett, 2009, chapter 9). S/he is also a third ecologist who gains their livelihood sustainably from, and with, the living earth.

Living earth

Symbiosis is a fact of evolution: no evolution without symbiosis. Symbiosis is a factor in evolution: species evolve through symbiosis with other species. It is also a factor in bioregions, and bioregionalism. Charles Darwin's theory of evolution by natural selection was not possible without bioregions and symbiosis. This theory was a Copernican Revolution in biology that ranks alongside the Marxian revolution in political economy and the Freudian revolution in psychology. All three decentred human subjectivity. Louis Althusser (1984, pp. 170–171) acknowledged the pivotal role of Freud and Karl Marx while overlooking Darwin. He argued that:

> Not in vain did Freud sometimes compare the critical reception of his discovery with the upheavals of the Copernican Revolution. Since Copernicus, we have known that the earth is not the 'centre' of the universe. Since Marx, we have known that the human subject, the economic, political or philosophical ego is not the 'centre' of history – . . . that history has no centre. . . . In turn, Freud has discovered for us that the real subject, the individual in his real essence, has not the form of the ego, centred on the 'ego', on 'consciousness' or on 'existence' – . . . that the human subject is de–centred, constituted by a structure which has no 'centre' either, except in the imaginary misrecognition of the 'ego', that is, in the ideological formations in which it 'recognizes' itself.

Principally the subject misrecognizes itself in its narcissistic reflection in the fetishized commodity in which the consuming subject recentres itself (or more precisely finds itself recentred) as the addressee of (or is recentred by) every advertisement, every mass–produced message.

To Freud and Marx as the decenterers of psychic and productive human subjectivity Darwin needs to be added as the decenterer of embodied and biological human subjectivity. Since Darwin 'Man' no longer occupies, as William Godfrey-Smith (1979, p. 317; my emphasis) puts it, 'a *biologically* privileged position.' 'Man,' however, continues to occupy a culturally privileged position in the production of commodities from raw materials supplied by the earth, in the consumption of fetishized commodities manufactured from those materials and in the expulsion of pollutants and wastes back into the earth-household.

Yet whereas Freud, Marx and Darwin were decentring the subject psychologically, productively and biologically, Henry Ford and John Wanamaker were recentring the subject in consumption in a counter-Copernican revolution. Since Wanamaker, the leading founder of the American department store, the consuming subject has been reinstituted as the centre of his or her own consumptive world. Since Ford, the inventor not only of the assembly line and mass production but also of mass consumption, the subject consuming the commodities of industrial technology (especially the car) is the centre of the history of modernity (however alienated the individual producer may be). The consumer is the centred subject of every commodity, the addressee of every shop window display, every advertisement, every fashion catwalk, every cinema, every film, every television set and show, every computer monitor. The consuming subject is a desiring subject whose desires are repressed and sublimated in and by semiosis and consumption. Desire for Deleuze and Guattari (1977, p. 26) 'lacks a fixed subject; there is no fixed subject unless there is repression.' And its counterpart sublimation I would add.

Besides the Copernican revolution in subjectivity brought about by Marx, Freud and Darwin a Copernican revolution in ecology was wrought by Ernst Haeckel, Peter Kropotkin and Elen Swallow (see Giblett, 2011) that saw the embodied subject as not only a biological being with no special privileges, but also as the member of a community of living beings and non-living things with responsibilities. Since Leopold, the embodied subject is, or should be, a member of a biological community, not the owner of land as property or a consumer of commodities as fetishes. Humans should not only be part of a cultural community but also good citizens of a natural community. According to Leopold (1949, p. 204), a

> land ethic simply enlarges the boundaries of the community to include soils, waters, plants and animals, or collectively: the land . . . a land ethic changes the role of *Homo sapiens* from conqueror of the land community to plain member and citizen of it.

The land ethic also changes the relationship to the land from mastery to mutuality and the role of the land from commodity to community. Godfrey-Smith (1979, pp. 314, 317) comments that 'land in Leopold's view is not a commodity which belongs to us, but a community to which we belong' where a community is construed as 'a collection of individuals who engage in cooperative behaviour to their mutual benefit.' Whereas the counter-Copernican revolution in capitalist consumption has triumphed, the Copernican revolution in land community has not yet had its day.

Darwin decentred the embodied subject as biological being but his theory of 'the survival of the fittest' and 'the struggle for existence' was centred in the urban and industrial capitalist 'jungle' rather than in the tropical rainforest. In a letter to Engels, Marx critiqued Darwin for, in the words of Keith Thomas (1984, p. 90),

> representing the natural world of the animal kingdom as one of free competition and for seeing among the beasts and plants his own English society, 'with its division of labour, competition, opening up of new markets, "inventions" and the Malthusian "struggle for existence"'.

Yet 'free competition' is never a level playing field on which all players are treated equally and the game is played fairly, just as 'free trade' is not fair trade. There are 'winners and losers,' and violence, as Walter Benjamin argued in 1921, is the only other means besides natural selection for Darwin by which winners win and losers lose. Darwin's biology for William Benjamin (1979, p. 133, 1996, p. 237), 'in a thoroughly dogmatic manner, regards violence as the only original means, besides natural selection, appropriate to all the vital ends of nature.' Violence becomes the *sine qua non* of nature, but the violence Darwin saw in nature was cultural, or to be more precise, the violence of modern industrial capitalism projected onto nature. Darwin for Roszak (1992, p. 155) 'read the ethos of industrial capitalism into the jungle.' The jungle was then used to support the ideology of industrial capitalism. Nature confirmed culture, as it did in landscape aesthetics and the gentleman's park estate.

The Social Darwinists took the law of the jungle and applied it to industrial capitalism and the urban jungle, but Darwin had already taken the law of industrial capitalism and the urban jungle and applied it to the tropical rainforest. Biologists such as Tim Low (2002, especially pp. 112, 115 and 122) who use the Social Darwinian law in which 'winners prosper and losers disappear' to describe the way in which some species survive in human modified environments whereas others become extinct close the circle. But late in the day Low (2002, p. 280) at the end of his book charges that 'one of the worst eco-crimes we commit is helping winners displace losers.' The trope returns full circle to consume its own tail (tale) like the uroborus. Industrial capitalism was an urban jungle of the 'survival of the fittest' that Darwin read into the rainforest. The urban and extra-urban jungle in which 'winners prosper and losers disappear' reads Darwinism onto industrial capitalism.

Certainly there is competition in nature but there is also cooperation. Nature can be 'red in tooth and claw' as it was for Tennyson, though this projects the sadistic (especially oral sadistic) features of industrial capitalism and the urban 'jungle' on to nature. All those orally sadistic monsters (including dinosaurs) of Hollywood films and American and British television are projections of industrial capitalist oral sadism and its monstrous machines that are used to justify and designed to deflect attention away from the latter. Nature is not only 'red in tooth and claw' but also green in leaf and branch.

Cooperation is as much a part of nature as competition, if not more so. For Kropotkin (1989, p. 6) 'mutual aid is as much a law of animal life as mutual struggle, but . . . as a factor of evolution, it most probably has a far greater importance.' Tim Flannery (1994, pp. 15, 84) has concurred that:

> evolution in Australia is not driven solely by nature 'red in tooth and claw.' Here, a more gentle force – that of coadaptation – is important. . . . It is cooperation rather than competition which has been selected for in many Australian environments.

For Kropotkin (1989, pp. 30, 60), 'the war of each against all is not *the* law of nature. . . . Life is struggle; and in that struggle the fittest survive' but the fittest (the survivors) are those who are the most cooperative, not the most competitive. The Hobbesian war of each against all was a projection of Thomas Hobbes's royalist reaction to the terrors of the English Civil War onto the state of nature in order to justify and legitimate restoration of the monarchy. The law of nature is each with all, for each is all.

The most mutually symbiotic survive. Symbiosis strictly considered only occurs between living things; living things in order to live require other living things. As William Trager (1970, p. 1) puts, 'no organism lives alone.' No 'man,' or woman, or child, or plant, or animal, is an island, as John Donne said. Yet for an organism to live, it not only requires other organisms, but also the life-supporting habitats or bioregions in which those other organisms live, and so in which it lives. Those bioregions for all species, however microscopic, are made up of intricately interweaving and interconnecting exchanges of matter which sustain life. So intertwined are these relationships that it is ultimately impossible to separate out an organism from its habitat. In a sense an organism is, or is the product and producer of, its habitat. This habitat, this bioregion is living, and bioregions live with other bioregions in a living whole breathing in air, rooted in earth, drinking water.

This idea of earth as living organism, rather than as dead matter, is by no means new. R. G. Collingwood (1945, pp. 31, 95) found it in the ancient Greeks (for further discussion see Giblett, 2011, chapter 1). It is there too in the work of P. D. Ouspensky (1951, pp. 178–191) in his key words of 'animated nature,' 'a living earth' and '"dead-nature" lives' as 'some gigantic [though not gargantuan or monstrous] organism.' The work of V. I. Vernadsky (1945, pp. 1–12), the inventor of the concept of the bio-sphere, is credited by Jeremy Rifkin (1991, p. 258) with being 'the first modern acknowledgment of earth as a living organism.' It may be more precise to see Vernadsky as the first *post*modern acknowledgement and Henry David Thoreau as the first modern acknowledgement. For Thoreau (1962, *VI*, p. 121), nearly a hundred years before Vernadsky, 'the earth is all alive.' For us, too, today, humans need to (re-learn to) live with the earth as living being.

The symbiocene

Psycho-symbiosis nurtures earthly sacrality and develop ways of living bio- and psycho-symbiotic livelihoods in bioregions of the living earth in the symbiocene, the hoped-for age superseding the Anthropocene. The Anthro-pocene is also Anthropobscene, a laying bare of the wastes and pollutants that modern industrial capitalism and its technologies wanted the -ospheres (atmosphere, hydrosphere, biosphere, etc.) to hide. The symbiocene is the paradigm of mutuality posed against the failed paradigm of mastery of the anthropocentric (see Giblett, 2011, especially figure 2, pp. 32–34). The Anthropocene can be defined as the geological age of the laying and layer-ing up and down of anthropogenic strata in the pollution of land, waters and air, and the heating up of all three in the new, disrupted (and disruptive) arrangement of the four elements and the four seasons (see Giblett, 2013, chapter 18). These anthropogenic strata are what Serres calls 'plaque tec-tonics' in which 'a great many humans form a "plaque," a formation that *disturbs* [the] functioning [of physical communality] . . . *plaques* of physi-cal *scoria* of humans . . . are encrusted upon and overlap the globe' (cited by Conley, 1997, p. 65; see also Serres, 1995, p. 16). These plaques of human-ity are reshaping the globe, like plate tectonics, and 'the Earth is quaking anew,' as Serres (1995, p. 86) puts it, in feral quaking zones, as I put it (see Giblett, 2009, chapter 1).

The Anthropocene came out of the economic politics of mercantile capi-talism, industrial capitalism, enclosure of the commons, private property, the commodity market and the feral quaking zone. The Anthropocene came out of its drive for, and the failed paradigm of, mastery. The anthropogenic stratigraphic layers of the Anthropocene gave rise to what Bruno Latour calls 'the New Climate Regime' in which 'there is no longer any question of "mastering" nature' (Latour, 2017, pp. 111–115). Rather, 'nature' is mastering, or monstering, us. The new, anthropogenic climate regime rules – and it is *not* okay. The Anthropocene is also Anthropobscene, a laying bare of the wastes and pollutants that modern industrial capitalism and its technologies wanted the -ospheres (atmosphere, hydrosphere, biosphere, etc.) to hide.

The symbiocene can be defined as the geological age of the laying and layering up and down of bodies of land, waters, air, beings and things in biogenic and non-biogenic strata, and the inter-corporeal relationship of loving union between them in the feral and native quaking zones (see Giblett, 2009, chapter 1). The symbiocene comes out of the economic politics of the commons, compassion for all beings, mutual aid, the carnivalesque marketplace (not the capitalist market) and the native quaking zone. The symbiocene comes out of its love for, and paradigm of, mutuality.

As ever, Thoreau was there before anyone else when he wrote in the mid-nineteenth century with stunning prophetic insight (foresight) in *Walden*, the old testament of conservation, that:

> The earth is not a mere fragment of dead history, stratum upon stratum like the leaves of a book, to be studied by geologists and antiquaries chiefly, but living poetry like the leaves of a tree, which precede flowers and fruit – not a fossil earth, but a living earth; compared with whose great central life all animal and vegetable life is merely parasitic.
>
> (Thoreau, 1997, p. 289)

The earth is not an object to be studied by geologists alone who preside over the dead strata of the Anthropocene and by antiquaries, such as Muir, who study the dead strata of the fossil earth like leaves in a book holy or otherwise. The earth is not only layers of capitalist crud laid up and down in the land, waters and air from the burning of fossil fuels and the manufacturing and disposal of commodities in the Anthropocene. The earth is also a symbiotic body with a trunk and palms like leaves of a trees, a living poem in the symbiocene.

The symbiotic body of the earth comes out of the traditional cultures in which earth is body and/or the body is earth. It supersedes the machine body of modern Western medicine, the battlefield body of illness narratives, the grotesque body of the lower strata, the monstrous body of the slimy depths, the Fascist body of the war machine, the textual body of the surface of inscription, the sporting body imprisoned in the time-machine and the cyborg of the body-machine of the civilian soldier.[3] The symbiocene embraces these bodies in the body of the earth in which healthy bodies, minds, lands and waters can and do flourish in their bioregional and local home place of the living earth (see Giblett, 2006, 2008a, 2009, chapter 8, 2013). The stratigraphic symbiocene cuts across the biosphere, the ecosphere, the public and private spheres, the electro-magnetosphere that makes wireless telecommunication possible and the extra-terrestrial sphere where the communication satellites orbit. Transportation and communication technologies function in these spheres. They are the greater ambit of the earth-home (see Giblett, 2008b; 2011, chapter 2).

Making a connection to local place, its plants, animals and their seasonal changes, is a necessary response, and antidote, to the globalized world in which many people now live and work and which impacts on our lives in numerous ways. It is vital to think and act locally as well as globally. Connecting to local place can be a reclusive retreat into a smaller, narrower and safer world away from the incursions of the bigger, badder global world. But it is also a way of acknowledging and respecting the interconnectedness of all life from the local to the global and back again. Our lives are lived locally (if not also globally) and are dependent on local air, water and food mainly supplied from within and by our bioregional home-habitat. We have aerials and cables, but we also have roots – however shallow or transient they may be. We feed off nutrients in the soil and although we may up roots and change soil occasionally or frequently, we are still putting down them into a soil, drinking local water, breathing the air around us and largely eating local food. That air and soil has a history, a human and a natural history. Knowing its composition enriches our lives and helps to connect us to the other living beings living in the same soil. That sense of mutuality between people and place is vital to conserving a place and the planet.[4]

All living creatures – plants and animals, human and non-human – live in a bioregion, a catchment or watershed, and an air-shed with its unique suite of plants and animals. The bioregion is the place of home, the home place. All creatures are dependent and impact on their bioregion to greater or lesser extent, with longer or shorter term damaging and/or rehabilitating effects. The relationship between creatures and their bioregion (and ultimately the earth and the biosphere) takes place on a continuum from the parasitic to the symbiotic through the inquilinistic (in which one party shares the home of another without significant disadvantage to the homeowner, such as normally the embryo *in-utero*; see Giblett, 2011, chapter 12). This continuum is not only biological and bio-geographical, but also psychological and spiritual (see also Giblett, 2011, chapter 12).

The bioregion is home not only to biological creatures, but also to spiritual, even mythological, creatures who are emanations and expressions of the place and its processes. They are the spirits of the place, the *genii loci*.

The 'spirit of a place' is a being, not a feeling; it is a way of being, and a way of living. Marsh monsters and swamp serpents and other monstrous figures, such as fiery dragons and earthy/watery alligators and crocodiles, are such creatures. Rather than regarding them with horror and demonizing them as evil beings, they should be respected and revered as creatures of the sacred earth. Long may they live; long may other creatures live with them. Please help conserve them and their homes of places on, under and above the earth. After all, it is their – and our – only home.

Notes

1 I discuss the possibility of the sustainable city (and make some proposals for it) in Giblett (2009, chapter 3, 2016, chapter 15).
2 The word 'physically' is added to the later version.
3 Each of these bodies receives a chapter-by-chapter treatment in Giblett (2008a).
4 For my bioregional connection to the local place where I lived for 30 years, see Giblett (2006, 2013).

References

Abercrombie, M., M. Hickman, M. Johnson and M. Thain (1990). *Symbiosis, in The New Penguin Dictionary of Biology*, 8th edition, London: Penguin, pp.542–543.

Althusser, L. 1984. *Essays on Ideology*, B. Brewster, trans. London: Verso.

Benjamin, J. 1990. *The Bonds of Love: Psychoanalysis, Feminism, and the Problem of Domination*. London: Virago.

Benjamin, W. 1979. *One Way Street and Other Writings*, E. Jephcott and K. Shorter, trans. London: New Left Books.

Benjamin, W. 1996. *Selected Writings: Volume 1, 1913–1926*, M. Bullock and M. Jennings, eds. Cambridge, MA: The Belknap Press of Harvard University Press.

Collingwood, R. 1945. *The Idea of Nature*. London: Oxford University Press.

Conley, V. 1997. *Ecopolitics: The Environment in Poststructuralist Thought*. London and New York: Routledge.

Deleuze, G. and F. Guattari. 1977. *Anti-Oedipus: Capitalism and Schizophrenia*, R. Hurley, M. Seem and H. Lane, trans. New York: Viking Press.

Flannery, T. 1994. *The Future Eaters: An Ecological History of the Australasian Lands and People*. Chatswood, NSW: Reed.

Giblett, R. 2006. *Forrestdale: People and Place*. Bassendean: Access Press.

Giblett, R. 2008a. *The Body of Nature and Culture*. Basingstoke: Palgrave Macmillan.

Giblett, R. 2008b. *Sublime Communication Technologies*. Basingstoke: Palgrave Macmillan.

Giblett, R. 2009. *Landscapes of Culture and Nature*. Basingstoke: Palgrave Macmillan.

Giblett, R. 2011. *People and Places of Nature and Culture*. Bristol: Intellect Books.

Giblett, R. 2013. *Black Swan Lake: Life of a Wetland*. Bristol: Intellect Books.

Giblett, R. 2016. *Cities and Wetlands: The Return of the Repressed in Nature and Culture.* London: Bloomsbury.

Godfrey-Smith, W. 1979. The Value of Wilderness. *Environmental Ethics*, 1, pp. 309–319.

Klein, Milton. 1980. On Mahler's Autistic and Symbiotic Phases: An Exposition and Evaluation, *Psychoanalysis and Contemporary Thought*, 4(1), pp. 69–105.

Kropotkin, P. 1989. *Mutual Aid: A Factor in Evolution.* Montreal: Black Rose Books.

Latour, B. 2017. *Facing Gaia: Eight Lectures on the New Climate Regime.* Cambridge: Polity.

Leopold, A. 1949. *A Sand County Almanac and Sketches Here and There.* New York: Oxford University Press.

Low, T. 2002. *The New Nature.* Camberwell: Penguin.

Mahler, M. 1952. On Child Psychosis and Schizophrenia: Autistic and Symbiotic Infantile Psychoses. *The Psychoanalytic Study of the Child*, 7, pp. 286–305.

Mahler, M. 1968. *On Human Symbiosis and the Vicissitudes of Individuation, Volume 1, Infantile Psychosis.* New York: International Universities Press.

Mahler, M. 1972. On the First Three Sub-Phases of the Separation-Individuation Process, *International Journal of Psychoanalysis*, 53, pp. 333–338.

Mahler, M. and M. Furer. 1966. Development of Symbiosis, Symbiotic Psychosis, and the Nature of Separation Anxiety. . . . *International Journal of Psychoanalysis*, 47, pp. 559–560.

Mahler, M., F. Pine and A Bergman. 1975. *The Psychological Birth of the Human Infant*: Symbiosis and Individuation. New York: Basic Books.

Margulis, L. 1971. Symbiosis and Evolution. *Scientific American*, 225, pp. 49–57.

Margulis, L. 1981. *Symbiosis in Cell Evolution: Life and Its Environment on the Early Earth.* San Francisco: W. H. Freeman.

Margulis, L. 1998. *Symbiotic Planet: A New Look at Evolution.* New York: Basic Books.

Ouspensky, P. 1951. *Tertium Organum: The Third Canon of Thought: A Key to the Enigmas of the World*, third edition. N. Bessaraboff and C. Bragdon, trans. New York: Alfred A. Knopf.

Plumwood, V. 1993. *Feminism and the Mastery of Nature.* London: Routledge.

Rifkin, J. 1991. *Biosphere Politics: A New Consciousness for a New Century.* New York: Crown.

Roszak, T. 1992. *The Voice of the Earth.* London: Bantam.

Sale, K. 1985. *Dwellers in the Land: The Bioregional Vision.* San Francisco: Sierra Club Books.

Serres, M. 1982. *The Parasite*, L. Schehr trans. Baltimore: The Johns Hopkins University Press.

Serres, M. 1995. *The Natural Contract*, E. MacArthur and W. Paulson, trans. Ann Arbor: University of Michigan Press.

Stern, D. 1985. *The Interpersonal World of the Infant: A View from Psychoanalysis and Developmental Psychology.* New York: Basic.

Thomas, K. 1984. *Man and the Natural World: Changing Attitudes in England 1500–1800*. Harmondsworth: Penguin.

Thoreau, H. 1962. *The Journal of Henry D. Thoreau, Volumes I-XIV*, B. Torrey and F. Allen, eds. New York: Dover.

Thoreau, H. 1997. *Walden*. Boston: Beacon.

Trager, W. 1970. *Symbiosis*. New York: Van Nostrand Reinhold.

Vernadsky, W. 1945. The Biosphere and the Noösphere. *American Scientist*, 33, pp. 1–12.

Warming, E. 1909. *Oecology of Plants: An Introduction to the Study of Plant Communities*. Oxford: Clarendon Press.

Index

For Product Safety Concerns and Information please contact our EU
representative GPSR@taylorandfrancis.com
Taylor & Francis Verlag GmbH, Kaufingerstraße 24, 80331 München, Germany